Roddy,
So glad to re-connect with you and Janie. Hope we can continue our old friendship on a regular basis.
Hope you enjoy the book!

From one good glove man to another.
Jerry

THAT EMPTY FEELING

THE REAL STORY OF ONE 72-HOUR RESCUE MISSION INTO LAOS

Terry P. Arentowicz

AuthorHouse™ LLC
1663 Liberty Drive
Bloomington, IN 47403
www.authorhouse.com
Phone: 1-800-839-8640

© 2013 Terry P. Arentowicz. All rights reserved.

No part of this book may be reproduced, stored in a retrieval system, or transmitted by any means without the written permission of the author.

Published by AuthorHouse   12/05/2013

ISBN: 978-1-4918-3625-5 (sc)
ISBN: 978-1-4918-3627-9 (hc)
ISBN: 978-1-4918-3626-2 (e)

Library of Congress Control Number: 2013920714

Any people depicted in stock imagery provided by Thinkstock are models, and such images are being used for illustrative purposes only.
Certain stock imagery © Thinkstock.

This book is printed on acid-free paper.

Because of the dynamic nature of the Internet, any web addresses or links contained in this book may have changed since publication and may no longer be valid. The views expressed in this work are solely those of the author and do not necessarily reflect the views of the publisher, and the publisher hereby disclaims any responsibility for them.

TABLE OF CONTENTS

Acknowledgements vii
Dedication xi
Foreword xiii

Chapter 1.   Uncle Ho's Neighborhood 1
Chapter 2.   What The Hell is SOG? 8
Chapter 3.   Flying the Friendly Skies 17
Chapter 4.   Joseph's Silver Wings 28
Chapter 5.   Good Pilots Too 44
Chapter 6.   Jolly 26 Return to Base 54
Chapter 7.   Flying on Fumes 65
Chapter 8.   Not a Day Goes By 75
Chapter 9.   Nice Doggy 98
Chapter 10. Let There Be Light 131
Chapter 11. 70 Pounds of Molten Metal 139
Chapter 12. That's a Negative 162
Chapter 13. Steak and Eggs 172
Chapter 14. De' ja Vu All Over Again 178

Awards Resulting From Action on Hill 891, Laos, 1967 191
Glossary 193
Bibliography 197

ACKNOWLEDGEMENTS

Because little has been written about the "secret war" conducted in Laos and Cambodia, That Empty Feeling, has relied on eyewitness accounts. Both the Special Forces soldiers who fell under SOG's command, and the pilots and their crews who supported SOG operations, were all gracious and generous to the author.

The sharing of personal thoughts, memoirs, flight logs and anecdotes formed the foundation for That Empty Feeling. I thank you all for allowing me the privilege to tell the true story of what must have been a most challenging period of your lives.

Russell Berger, Medic U.S.A.—interview
Ron Bock, Special Forces—interview, memoirs, photo
Bob Cavanaugh, Special Forces—interview, letters
Vern Dander, Pilot U.S.A.F.—interview, memoirs
Cletus Farmer, Pilot U.S.A.—memoirs
Lloyd Fisher, Special Forces—interview, memoirs
Wayne Fisk, U.S.A.F.—speech
Alan Fleming, SOG, interview, memoirs
Paul Gregoire, Pilot U.S.M.C.—memoirs
David Hagler, Major U.S.A.—memoirs
Joseph Hanner, Pilot U.S.M.C.—memoirs, flight log
James Kilbourne, Pilot U.S.A.F., interview
Corwin Kippenhan, Pilot U.S.A.F.—interview, flight log
Jack McTasney, Pilot U.S.A.F.—interview, memoirs
Don Monk, Pilot U.S.A.—memoirs
Ira Taylor, Pilot U.S.A.—memoirs
Bill Vowell, SOG—interview, memoirs

Terry Whitney—interview, photos
Kent Woolridge, Pilot U.S.A.—interview, memoirs
William Zanow, Pilot U.S.A.—interview

Other contributors
Dr. Joan Baker, Forensic Anthropologist—interview
Star Barkman, Graphic Artist—sketches
Heidi Prudente, cover photo
John Trabachino, editing

Special Acknowledgements
Gamble Dick—Thank you for your time and encouragement when it was most needed, and for educating me on the "ways" of Special Forces and SOG operations. It is easy to understand why Gamble's fellow soldiers found him to be an outstanding leader and a caring person.

Linda Arentowicz—Thank you for all the support on this book project, and for all you have been to me for 43 years.

"Another kind of war, new in its intensity, ancient in its origin—war by guerrilla, subversives, insurgents, assassins, war by ambush instead of by combat, by infiltration instead of by aggression, seeking victory by eroding and exhausting the enemy instead of engaging him."

President John J. Kennedy 1962

WW II grave marker at Monte Casino, Italy. A mother's sentiment and universal feeling for every son that gave their life for others. Photo courtesy of George T. Cerrigone.

DEDICATION

To the men who gave the most "precious gift, an un-lived life," and to those whose Herculean rescue efforts would lead their souls to unrest; to Recon Team Flatfoot, Hatchet Force Bulldog, the Covey FACs and the pilots and crews of the Jolly Greens, VNAF Kingbees, Sandies, Army Huey's and Marine Helos, whose missions were purposely forgotten and conveniently denied by our own country. There are not enough medals, ribbons, or decorations to bestow that could possibly fill the emptiness. A simple "thank you" now rings hollow. Time has failed to erase the memories.

FOREWORD

Chester, NJ 0900, 30 May, 2005

The Chester Borough Police had secured both ends of Main Street which allowed the growing crowd to wander leisurely across the normally busy County Road 513, Dover Chester Road. Most of the visitors milled around the shrouded statue that was to be the subject of the Memorial Day dedication. A couple of hundred meters east of town the baseball field, nearly as old as Abner Doubleday himself, now served as a staging area for a variety of organizations that would enter town to participate in an old fashioned small town event. There were no aspiring "Mickey Mantle" shagging fly balls on the thick green grass on this day.

The outfield was occupied by musicians in blue plaid kilts limbering not their throwing arms but their bag pipes, drums, and horns. Their Columbia blue dress shirts carried the familiar inverted gold triangle with the N.J. State Police clearly marked inside. The leather belts that supported their side arms were highly shined, and their haircuts were high and tight. Each musician tuned up their instruments individually, and finally, as a group their mournful notes floated in the direction of town. The songs were a harbinger of the seriousness this special Memorial Day would bring.

Colonel Rick Fuentes, who commanded the New Jersey State Police, had arranged for the NJSP Pipe and Drum Band to perform. Always professional, the pipes requested were a welcome site compared to a view of a trooper in a rear view mirror on the Parkway. Fuentes was friends with one of the rescuers from Hill 891, things often work this way.

A contingent of U.S.A.F. Pararescue men (P.J.s) gathered along the right field foul line. Several talked on hand held radios to an incoming Air Force UH-60 rescue helicopter (piloted by Lieutenant Colonel Mike

Noyes and orchestrated on the ground by Sergeant Jules Roy) that would perform a fly over. Jump boots, bloused trousers, silver wings and maroon berets were the hard earned calling cards of the Air Force's only elite unit. Most of these "P.J.s" had not yet been born when the subject of the memorial dedication, Sergeant Larry W. Maysey, had been killed somewhere in Southeast Asia in 1967. They had driven many miles to pay their respects to one of their own regardless of the difference in the era. Soon they too would be placed in harms way in Iraq or Afghanistan, some in both and some more than once.

For a little more than a year Staff Sergeant Leonidas Villanueva had been empowered by the U.S. Air Force to form a competitive drill team. The Air Force was never known for close order drill or marching, yet Sergeant Villanueva forged ahead to produce a very fine product. The Air Force would handle the gun salute in honor of Air Force Pararescue man Larry W. Maysey. The colors would be presented by the Chester Volunteer Fire Department and Post 342 of the American Legion. A light breeze quickly brought the flags to life. The senior of the two teams was clearly the Legionnaires whose silver hair peeked out from beneath their overseas caps. The antique store porches began to fill with young women in sun dresses, some with their children in tow. They competed for elbow room with leashed Labrador retrievers, and senior citizens wrestling with their unruly lawn chairs.

The weather had been rainy for days hampering the preparation and construction at the Memorial site. But this day was perfect, and it was shaping up to be a truly Main Street U.S.A. event, the kind that only Norman Rockwell could put on canvas convincingly. It was a throwback to a time that had long since passed.

The event had taken two years to prepare. Larry Maysey Veteran's Committee left no stone unturned on behalf of their fallen classmate and friend. Nearly 38 years had passed since Sergeant Larry W. Maysey had been killed in action somewhere in Southeast Asia, presumed to be South Vietnam. The Air Force had released only the sketchiest of details, so the dearth of information added to the family's grief. Rumor and speculation circulated between the town's luncheonettes and bars. The prevailing rumor had Maysey as a prisoner held somewhere in North Vietnam, although the rumors were as numerous as the diners and "hoppers" that frequented the small town's greasy spoons and watering holes.

Memorial Day flyover (2005), piloted by Lieutenant Colonel Michael Noyes. "Jolly" spews green smoke in honor of Sergeant Larry W. Maysey. Photo courtesy of David Dean.

What is known is that the Air Force had seen fit to select Maysey to join the ranks of their elite program known as pararescuemen. The cross training was a murderous 18 month program admiringly referred to as the "pipeline." As the years slipped by, and the nation did its best to develop amnesia when it came to recognizing both the living and the dead warriors from Vietnam, only a trickle of information did reach Maysey's family and friends. He had been killed in a rescue attempt along with co-pilot Ralph Brower and flight mechanic Eugene L. Clay. Also on board the ill-fated helo were two Special Forces members, Joseph Kussick and Bruce Baxter. None of the bodies of the five were ever returned to their families.

This Memorial Day had been set aside to honor and recognize one of Chester's favorite sons. The town had pulled out all the stops and nature had provided a Rockwellian Day. The tiny hamlet had once been surrounded by dairy farms, orchards, and iron ore mines. It had once welcomed back the 15th New Jersey Volunteers, an infantry regiment that served with distinction at Fredericksburg and Chancellorsville. The 15th had done their share of dying and some of their ranks had been subjected to imprisonment by the Confederates at Andersonville, a fate some felt was worse than death. The grave sites of local men who had served with the 15th were interred on Hillside Avenue. Those men, along with numerous Revolutionary and Korean War dead, along with a strong contingent from World War II, stood a silent vigil from their hillside graves overlooking the newly constructed Maysey dedication site. The town had also opened its arms to their share of W.W. II veterans who had participated in D-Day, and to those who found their way to the bloody campaigns in the Pacific. Some of these vets participated in the Memorial Day ceremony. Most recently, an old rumor had been rekindled, claiming a mass grave existed containing Revolutionary war dead. It is now being looked into.

Downtown, the crowd swelled into the thousands, easily exceeding the resident population and spilling off the sidewalks and on to the street. The Committee all wondered what mood would prevail. The crowd chose—it would be a serious celebration. If they had voted, it could not have been a better choice.

The Reverend Scott Hoffman organized the line of march at the edge of the baseball field. He was Larry Maysey's step brother, a committee member and was savvy in the ways of small towns. He had promised a fair weather prayer and he was obviously in good with the Lord. Through his bullhorn he skillfully placed each organization into line without ruffling a single feather and soon the drums and pipes of the New Jersey State Police came to life and stepped off towards the waiting crowd. As the colors entered town, the crowd simultaneously stood and remained so until the last Cub Scout and Brownie had passed, Rockwell would have loved it.

The flag salute was followed by the Reverend's invocation and then several politicians, both local and state, addressed the crowd. Each of the dignitaries was brief and effective. The keynote speaker was Retired Chief Master Sergeant Wayne Fisk. His message proved to be both poignant and tear evoking. His message was aimed squarely at Sergeant Maysey's sacrifice and devotion. Fisk skillfully acknowledged the present day P.J.s and their own sacrifices. It was an obvious attempt to salute veterans from all eras.

A P.J. himself, Fisk had trained with Maysey and served five tours in Southeast Asia. He had also participated in the *Son Tay Prison Rescue Mission*, the most daring operation of the Vietnam War. He was awarded a Silver Star for his participation, and the day after Memorial Day he was to fly to Alabama to be entered into the Legion of Merit, most often reserved for officers. At 60, Fisk still looked like he could chew nails and gargle razor blades. His speech sparked interest in the big picture and questions were raised about Maysey's death on Hill 891 in Laos. Why were they in neutral Laos? Who else was there? Why did they not return?

The facts surrounding Sergeant Maysey's death began to take form when Wayne Fisk stepped to the dais. Fisk was privy to the secret war in Laos and Cambodia. The war had long since ended, yet information had still not reached, or had been available to most Americans. Only someone who had flown into the chaos many times could weave the realism and fear of a story. It was clear Fisk had been there many times. Yet as the dedication day wore on, more information would become available on what was thought to be a simple rescue on Hill 891 turned out to be a mind boggling operation whose times and dates are still argued today.

As it turned out, Maysey was an Air Force certified hero but he was not alone and that was certainly news to Maysey's family and friends. In addition to the Jolly Green Maysey had been aboard, there were aircraft from the U.S. Army, U.S. Air Force, Marines and VNAF (Vietnamese Air Force). The pilots and crews compiled an impressive record and many were heroes in their own right. As impressive as the air combat was, the Army Special Forces would headline 72 hours of bedlam and heroics. They, too, proved to be worthy of America's highest awards yet only a paltry number of those awards would ever be granted.

The following is Chief Master Sergeant Wayne Fisk's tribute to a fallen fellow P.J., Sergeant Larry W. Maysey.

"It is with great pleasure that I stand here on behalf of that elite group of men of which Larry Maysey was a part. Known as Pararescuemen—perhaps better known as PJs—we stand here today to celebrate the unveiling of this statue to the memory of this courageous American warrior, Larry W. Maysey."

"Like millions of Americans before him, in 1966 he interrupted his personal life and aspirations (because he had been taught well living in Chester) that it was his patriotic duty, his responsibility, as it is of all Americans, to defend this great land. Thus he followed in the footsteps of patriotic Americans before him who knew that each generation must perpetuate the ideals that America was founded upon; that freedom is granted only to those who defend it and are willing, if necessary, to die for its preservation. Larry knew his duty well.

"So he fulfilled it by joining the United States Air Force and (as a memorial in our nation's capitol to others of another time) states, "Not for reward or fame, not for place or rank, but in simple obedience to duty . . ." He was a man who stood out in masses of men. At boot camp he was immediately chosen for pararescue and was like all of us in 1966—confident, sure of himself and most anxious to go "nose-to-nose" with the bad guys in Vietnam.

"And, like all of us, he was formed into a PJ training team of many who, as the weeks and months of training passed, became fewer and fewer until only an elite, indefatigable, hard core of them remained.

"One of those men who remained and who was one of Larry's closest friends is here with us today. He is my teammate and brother PJ, Chief Master Sergeant (retired) Joseph "Stu" Stanaland. Chief Stanaland trained with Larry, went to war with Larry and was there when Larry was lost. Chief Stanaland (Stu) is our touchstone to the warrior who is the purpose for our gathering here today.

"I first met Larry in 1966 and we often saw each other until we both went to different PJ combat teams in Southeast Asia in 1967. He was a fine man and fine PJ.

"Larry and the pantheon of warriors of his ilk, like Stu, were unquestionably committed to the fulfillment of his mission, unquestionably brave in the face of the enemy and unquestionably a hero through his selfless act of courage.

"But the training that Larry underwent month after month in 1966 and 1967 did not alone instill in him that which came from the essence of his heart and made him what he was: a warrior who was to live by the Pararescue Code. The day Larry earned the privilege to wear the coveted maroon beret he assumed the dictates of the Pararescue Code, and it states:

"It is my duty as a Pararescueman to save life and aid the injured. I shall be prepared at all times to perform my assigned duties quickly and efficiently, placing these duties before all personal desires and comforts.

These things I do that others may live."

"No one can ever ask greater compliance of living by the code than did Larry. I have no doubt that someday an aging old PJ will bring his grandchild to this very spot and stand before this statue. And the child, after hearing the story of Larry will ask, "Grandfather, were you a hero like him?"

"The old PJ's eyes will assume a faraway look and they will mist over. His mind will flood with memories and travel back to a time of emergency beepers indicating the distress of downed airmen, and of soldiers and of Marines in enemy clutches.

In his mind's eye, he will once again see missiles and rockets flashing past his helicopter—so close that he could reach out and touch them. He will feel his frail craft being flung about by the explosive shock waves of enemy anti-aircraft artillery.

He will relive the anxiety and fear as bullets penetrate his aircraft, concerned as pieces are shredded and fall off into the jungle below. He will smell the explosive fumes of ruptured aviation fuel line and of burning electrical circuits.

But foremost in his mind he will remember the desperate radio calls of men under fire who are in a worse predicament than he. And he will know, once again, that there is no other place on earth for him to be than right here, right now, in this very moment of time.

He will reawaken the ferocity of battles in a very small and confined space, of men reaching out to him with the pleas and expectations of rescue on their lips and in their eyes.

He will recapture the memories of emerging hope as he places more and more of the men aboard his helicopter, and how that hope blossoms into elation and, then, finally triumph as they fly, battered and bleeding out of that God-forsaken hole of hell.

And when it is all over, when the ones he has been sent to rescue are in safe hands, he will remember the heartbreaking sadness of brothers at other times and other places that did not come back.

He will wipe his eyes and clear his throat and whisper proudly to that wonder struck child at his side, looking here at Larry, and he will answer "No I wasn't a hero like him—but I walked with men who were."

"We honor and remember Larry Maysey today in a sense that only a Merriam-Webster dictionary could define and which we are able to comprehend and agree with: He was "A man of great strength and courage, a man admired for his nobility and his exploits."

"The actions of this strong and courageous warrior are already legendary throughout our United States Air Force. Now, with the dedication of this memorial, the nobility of that legend will be known beyond the town limits of Chester, beyond the state lines of New Jersey and across the expanse of these United States. Such exploits cannot be confined.

"Yet this son of Chester, this hero of America, would be the first to correct me and all of us that he was not a hero, that he was only doing the job that he chose and for which he was trained.

"And he would point out that the true heroes are the ones who carry on after him and especially those who continue today and who are our defenders and our protectors. Larry would ask that in honoring him we look at these proud men and women here today in the fabric of our nation's military and salute and honor them as we would him.

"Like Larry they have stepped forward, not for reward or fame, not for place or rank, but in simple obedience to their duty. They are now our defenders of our American way of life.

"Larry fought in a war against a world threat of Communism. And that threat was defeated. Our defenders today, in the footsteps of such warriors as Larry, are fighting in another war, this time against a world threat of terrorism and fanaticism. And that threat, too, will be defeated because of them. (We can only hope Fisk was right.)

As you honor the exceptionality of Larry, his strength and his nobility, his exploits and his courage, then you must honor these fine men and women. For they, like Larry, answer a calling greater than themselves to a cause mightier than themselves. It is America.

"This, then and they are the legacy of Air Force Sergeant Larry W. Maysey: a son of Chester and a hero of America.

Thank you and God bless each of you; God bless Larry, and God bless America."

A collective sigh emerged from the audience and tears raced down the cheeks of even the most hardened veterans. The gut wrenching and emotional part was now over—it was time for pictures, hand shakes and some back slapping as well. Young PJs in shiny jump boots and maroon berets snapped photos of the Maysey statute and posed with the sculptor, Wayne Hyde, whose hands had truly captured the essence of a PJ. Hyde himself had lost a cousin in Vietnam. Without his talent and generous offer to work for a pittance, the Maysey Memorial would not have happened. The crowd, pleased with Hyde's artistic talent, hung around for some time. Many had supported the volunteer effort with generous donations and some had also loaned their special talents to the construction of the statue.

Many of the crowd retired to Hoffman Hall, the Chester Fire Department's "upstairs." The department's bar quickly sprang into action. The firemen were as adept at hosting a party as they were at dousing flames. The Air Force Drill Team (still in its infancy) performed an ad hoc show on the parquet dance floor before joining the civilians for adult beverages. Master Sergeant Leonides Villanueva kept a lid on things.

Through this happy hour a single individual emerged and introduced himself as "Gamble Dick." This of course, is a name you could not forget. He wanted to know if he could talk to Larry Maysey's relatives (only a few were still alive), a long lost friend, or maybe a reporter? He was a somewhat unremarkable figure, yet he seemed to be on a mission, not so much fact finding as fact providing. One got the impression he had been around. He was polished, in his late 50s early 60s, and he spoke with the assurance that might come with education and worldly experience. He had a brief sit down with Julia and Fritz Robinson, Larry Maysey's closest surviving relatives. They were Larry's legacy to his Chester roots.

Larry W. Maysey seen here prior to boarding an aircraft for a scuba jump, P.J. training 1966. Photo courtesy of Larry's Aunt, Mrs. Julia Robinson.

Gamble Dick claimed to have been on Hill 891 in Laos the very place Sergeant Larry W. Maysey had been killed in action. He had lead a 75 man Army Hatchet Force to 891, spent 2 hair-raising nights behind enemy lines and lived to tell about it. This Special Forces lead group had been sent to "clean up the mess" as one Green Beret Colonel had put it.

Was this guy for real? The book <u>Stolen Valor</u>, describes dozens of imposters claiming to have served in Vietnam and even wearing medals and awards they had bestowed on themselves. There was, however, no braggadocio in the message he delivered to Larry's Aunt and Uncle. He only wanted them to know that their nephew and his crew had not been abandoned and left alone, nor had they fallen into the hands of the NVA. This was not the message of an imposter. After all, he did not wear a boonie hat with a CIB (Combat Infantry Badge) pinned on or the ever present field jacket emblazoned with unit patches. (No beard and no Harley were in sight.) He seemed on the level.

Wayne Fisk (the key note speaker) had warned the Larry Maysey Veteran's Committee that he would not attend or participate without our assurance that all participants were exactly what they claimed to be. Although The Committee couldn't control who attended, they would use caution when it came to participants. Fisk himself knew of Gamble Dick and gave him a thumbs up on credibility. In describing Dick's unit and men, Fisk referred to them as "magnificent bastards." These "magnificent bastards" were actually U.S. Special Forces, Green Berets. Gamble Dick was the real deal. He had been on Hill 891. He knew the entire story. In short, he was a participant and eye witness with a sharp memory. He knew names, times, dates and had documented a lot of the events surrounding Hill 891 from those long lost days some 38 years ago. Yeah the guy in the plaid button down collar shirt had been there and done that. Dick had commanded a 75 man Hatchet Force for SOG (Studies and Observation Group.) True to the three letters, they studied, they observed, and they certainly were a group. Unbeknownst to most Americans in 1967, SOG took studying and observing just a little further, a lot further!

The saga begins with one lone Special Forces SOG recon team and within hours multiplied into a multi service operation so chaotic and helter skelter that even 40 years later the exact dates and times are disputed by the participants themselves.

What cannot be disputed is the incredible courage of all the participants involved. The Army Green Berets (SOG), Army helo pilots, Air Force helo pilots, FAC pilots, A1-E pilots, Marine air and all their crews along with the courageous efforts of the VNAF. At times the rescuers needed to be rescued and both human and material resources were expended non-stop for 72 hours.

The acts of bravery during this true saga would stir patriotism even in Jane Fonda's little black heart. Purple Hearts, Air Force Crosses, Silver Stars and the grand daddy of them all, a Medal of Honor, were bestowed, and rightly so. Had the event not taken place in Laos (a neutral country), awards for valor would most certainly have been pinned on more deserving chests. Brave men who survived to this day lament their inability to completely "win the day."

Forget the dope smoking image seen in Apocalypse Now and Platoon. Forget Sheen, Brando and Duval, Hill 891 had real heroes. They were unscripted and raw, and they laid it all on the line, and in some cases did it over and over again.

If there was ever any doubt in your mind about the commitment of American service men in Southeast Asia, this saga will make you a believer. So zip up your flight suit, check your survival gear and buckle your flight harness if you decide to fly into this chaos. You can even choose your aircraft: an A1-E Skyraider, a C-130, a Huey Slick, or a Jolly Green Giant HH3H. How about a slow moving FAC? You get motion sickness? In that case tag along with a Special Forces recon team or a SOG Hatchet Force. If you are going with these guys, check your web gear, clean your weapon and bring all the extra ammo you can "hump." You are going to need it! Oh, don't bother to bring C Rats—you should only be gone for the day.

South East Asia 1967

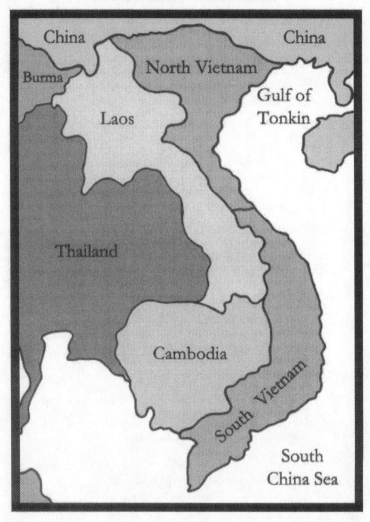

Sketch by Star Barkman.

CHAPTER 1

UNCLE HO'S NEIGHBORHOOD

It must be understood that all the events that took place on Hill 891 in Laos would never have transpired were it not for a system of trails and crude roads that had long been referred to as the "Truong Son Route." The North and South running trails took their names from a "similarly named mountain chain," How long the route had existed was anyone's guess, but modern times had seen the "route" take on a new moniker, The "Ho Chi Minh Trail."

Although secrecy always seemed to obscure the trails existence, it was destined for fame despite every effort to keep its very existence a secret. Like a giant emerald dining umbrella, the triple canopy jungle drooped down from ancient trees that towered from high above. Below the 80 to 90 foot trees the trails wound in serpentine fashion through two neutral countries, Laos and Cambodia. Fog and rain visited and revisited on a regular basis as if on cue from a Bella Lugosi film producer.

Cartographers seemed to have never visited this frontier wilderness yet by 1967 top American pilots found, bombed, strafed and napalmed the trail both day and night. Every conceivable type of aircraft was employed to stem the flow of troops and supplies sent by the North Vietnamese government flowing southward. U.S. pilots relished the "hunter killer" missions over the trail that at times offered a target rich environment. The air crews made many successful forays, yet the stubborn North Vietnamese continued to send their supplies and men despite taking losses from above. Indeed, even when U.S. boots touched the ground recon teams were stunned to see the volume of trucks and supplies continually heading south, bent on making war with their neighbors and with American troops.

Although the Trail ran clearly inside the borders of neutral Laos and Cambodia (see map), Ho Chi Minh was dedicated to preserving the quaint and rustic existence of the prime real estate he had cultivated. Like any charlatan East Coast realtor, Ho knew that "location" was everything, but he wasn't about to share any information with the public.

Ho's historical leadership reached all the way back to pre World War II Vietnam. Although his wispy goatee and folksy ways gave him the appearance that he was everyone's peasant uncle, in realty he was well travelled, highly informed and a master politician. His education included stops in France, England, China, the Soviet Union and possibly the U.S. as well. By 1967, Ho had already been a serious player in South East Asia, and as the 1960's progressed he would continue to put his stamp on world affairs.

Having sparred successfully with Japan during World War II, Ho then led the stunning defeat of the French at Dien Bien Phu. The elite French troops were defeated when the clever Northern forces under General Giap moved artillery pieces into the mountains on reinforced bicycles one piece at a time! French colonization had effectively been terminated. Unfortunately, the West still didn't acknowledge Ho Chi Minh's desire or resourcefulness as a leader.

"Uncle Ho" had weathered some great events in world history and had cultivated relationships with both Joseph Stalin and China's Mao Tse Tung. It wasn't clear which of the three most benefitted from the association. Whether Ho was a devout Communist prior to or after his meetings with his new friends is the subject of some debate. Clearly Ho benefitted from the coaching, financial support, and war materiel he received without which his goal of consolidating North and South Vietnam could never be realized.

Ho's PhD in political science was complete. He could cross either political or military swords with virtually anyone. His presidency in the north "Democratic Republic of Vietnam" only served to whet his patriotic appetite. Only the unification of North and South Vietnam would allow Ho to push away from the table. Ho's dream of a united Vietnam became America's nightmare as Communist influence around the world was on the rise. Alarmed that when one country fell to communist influence another was sure to follow (the domino theory), the U.S. began to form methods and strategies that would prevent Vietnamese unification.

Ho Chi Minh—A highly educated and savvy politician he successfully united North and South Vietnam. Sketch by Star Barkman.

The stage was now set for the peasant leader to match wits with America's Ivy League thinkers and intelligentsia. The cross hairs in Ho's political scope never wavered, and by 1959 North Vietnam began to support and nurture sympathizers in the south. The U.S. would be a foe unlike Japan or France. They were not interested in trade or economic gains that might be found in South East Asia. It was Ho's ideology American politicians opposed.

How could a poor country such as North Vietnam hope to impose its will on the south when the mightiest country in the world opposed it? Ho Chi Minh was going to have to be at his creative best. His political savvy would be tested over and over again. Neither Japan nor France could measure up to America's superior economy, much less the U.S. military machine. Ho's response to American superiority was nothing short of pure genius. Both Mao Tse Tung and Joseph Stalin could now take a lesson from their student. American Presidents Kennedy, Johnson and Nixon, along with their learned advisors and top generals, would find themselves bewildered by Ho Chi Minh.

As the U.S. and North Vietnam slowly engaged in what would be a long and epic struggle, Ho's methodology became adaptive and fluid. He made up his own rules yet seldom played by them. Nothing was out of bounds and his bag of tricks was beyond being deep. "We have to win independence at any cost, even if the Truong Son Mountains burn," and burn they would. It should not have come as a surprise to U.S. officials when Ho's northern army began to use a little known trail system that basically ran north and south. The Truong Son route was not within Vietnam's borders. It lay just slightly to the west of both North and South Vietnam. The route was obscure. At its best it compared to an Iowa farm road. At its worst it compared to a wild animal trail. The route's appeal to Ho was "location, location, location," it was just inside neutral Cambodia and Laos (see map). Ho turned the Trail's existence into a huge plus for his cause. His neighbors' neutrality not withstanding and his violation of international law seemed like only a small imposition on the powerless countries. Essentially, North Vietnam had invaded both Laos and Cambodia, although this strategy went unchallenged by the U.S. media and the rest of the world as well. Needless to say, neither Jane Fonda nor any college campus was seen protesting the North's aggression. Ho was dealing from the bottom of the deck, and his American counterparts seemed to receive one losing hand after another.

By 1959, North Vietnam was sending both men and materiel southbound and when questioned they simply denied it happened. Making improvements on the Trail allowed for an increased flow with each passing month, resulting in arms and ammunition reaching the "friendlies" in the south and the start of destabilizing of the south. The fact that the trail was inside sovereign countries was never in question. Everyone knew the trail and its surroundings were considered "Uncle Ho's Neighborhood." Traveling on or near it could be hazardous to your health. Ho's department of transportation employees not only carried shovels and rakes, but kept an AK-47 slung on their backs. These "Trail Keepers" made improvements to the roadway, grew vegetables and served as guides and security for the Northerners making their way south for the purpose of waging war on their neighbors. Of course the end result was to install a centralized government with a decidedly Communist flavor.

Ho initially readied a cadre of infiltrators who "wore untraceable peasant garb and carried captured French weapons." The north did not want to flaunt their presence on the trail and activity was kept to a minimal level. However, trail usage was only in its infancy in 1959. Utilizing 'sterile' soldiers did not go unnoticed and later the U.S. would turn the tables on the north with their own version of sterile soldiers.

The U.S. was aware of the north's duplicity on the trail but details of the activity were sketchy at best. The neutrality of both Laos and Cambodia coupled with the fecklessness of U.S. politicians ruled out how the U.S. might have handled the problem only a dozen years earlier during World War II. None of the old reliable remedies could be used. No Patton armor attack, no air drop by the 101st and the Marine specialty of amphibious assault were possible. Ho Chi Minh had eliminated all the easy answers and all it took was a little ingenuity and a lot of deceit. Ho had fired the opening salvos and the U.S. was clearly on the defensive. With the big stick answers ruled out the U.S. turned to the less obvious method of covert activity.

Ho Chi Minh Trail 1967

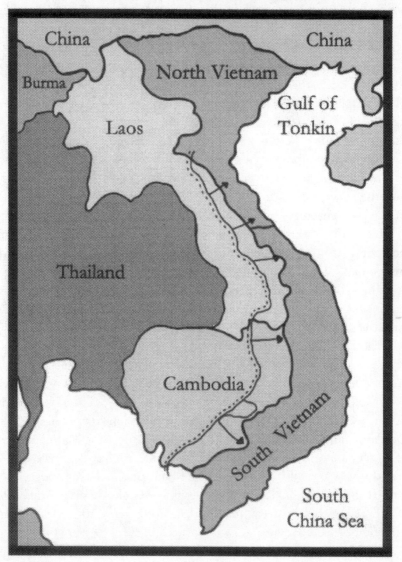

Sketch by Star Barkman.

The North Vietnamese could not be allowed to undermine U.S. interests in South Vietnam by simply using the "trail" as a means of transporting supplies via Cambodia and Laos. In response to Ho's trail usage, the CIA established a presence in Saigon, Republic of South Vietnam. Their mission was to discover just how significant the North's use of the trail had become. The CIA appointed William Colby to direct the mission. Colby had worked behind enemy lines during World War II and was espionage friendly. Colby was a bespectacled, bow tie wearing Ivy Leaguer as innocuous looking in America as Ho was in Vietnam.

Colby was familiar with working under restraints and actually was comfortable with the cloak and dagger approach. He came up with several ideas to gain information on Ho's trail usage. One of his first attempts was to employ left over French coffee planters to monitor North Vietnamese movement through Laos. Both the quantity and quality of the planter's reports were wanting. Colby was successful in convincing his superiors to allow American Special Forces personnel to train South Vietnamese to operate in Cambodia and Laos. Again, the attempt was not successful. Finally, an air infiltration group was readied but was deemed unready and cumbersome.

Colby's attempts at monitoring the North's trail activities met with more failure than success. However, it was apparent that the rate of trail usage was on the increase. Colby's first attempts only proved that he was in need of something that would provide more volume and detail on North Vietnam's increased activities. He needed something smart, not too visible, and possibly sinister as well.

It wasn't long before Colby and the CIA came up with yet another plan to track Ho's southern movements. This plan would place Americans directly in harm's way.

CHAPTER 2

WHAT THE HELL IS SOG?

What do you get when you combine S.F. (Special Forces) SOG (studies and observation group) and the CIA (Central Intelligence Agency)? The answer was exactly what William Colby needed to enter neutral Laos and Cambodia and monitor the Ho Chi Minh Trail and all that moved around it. The solution was as unique as the bow tie tucked beneath Mr. Colby's chin. Special Forces had been a part of the U.S. Army since 1952, and, their pedigree could be traced back to World War II. The modern mission statement for Special Forces fit Laos and Cambodia as snug as a Jane Fonda cocktail dress. Special reconnaissance along with guerilla warfare was already part of their dossier and training.

In 1961 President John F. Kennedy took an interest in Special Forces and seemed to have gained knowledge and foresight of guerilla warfare. He had connected the dots and felt that conventional forces alone could be successfully augmented by specially trained troops. He took special interest in S.F. and authorized the wearing of the Green Beret. The beret itself has been credited to Edson Raff, one of the first S.F. officers." J.F.K. then supplied the "juice" to remove the wraps from Special Forces, and who was going to argue with the popular young President? Suffice it to say that draining both serious N.C.O.s (non commissioned officers) and ear marking funds for S.F. that may have gone to the regular army was not always met with enthusiasm by the "old guard."

When Kennedy (in a speech) referred to the beret as a "symbol of excellence, a badge of courage and a mark of distinction in the fight for freedom," the Army Special Forces found a powerful ally and friend. Along about the same time, S.F. Sergeant Barry Saddler penned the

"Ballad of the Green Berets." It became a popular hit and was credited with raising public interest in Special Forces. Although John Wayne's movie "The Green Berets" may have been a bit over the top, it managed to put a positive spin on the noble mission of Special Forces. While ballads, movies and jaunty caps surely contributed to legend, they didn't help keep you alive or create any real success. To make the Special Forces really special, their training and education had to be specialized and in tune with their mission. This is where the S.F. parted ways with their parent organization, the regular Army. The average G.I. couldn't make it through S.F. training, nor would he be motivated to do so. According to Saddler's ballad, "one hundred men will test today, but only three wear the Green Beret." Whether Saddler's arithmetic was accurate really doesn't matter. It is safe to say only a small percentage ever realized their goal of wearing jump boots, silver wings, and the Green Beret.

Training began at Ft. Benning, Georgia, where both basic and infantry were combined into a fourteen week period. Following basic and infantry training, each and every S.F. candidate went on to a three week airborne school. The faint of heart found jumping out of perfectly functioning aircraft both mentally and physically challenging. Some candidates gave up their quest for a Green Beret at this juncture.

With jump school in the rear view mirror, training shifted to Fort Bragg, N.C. a.k.a. "John Wayne High School." Here the SOPC or Special Operations preparation course readied the candidate for what was known as "Phase I", a twenty-four day S.F. assessment and selection period. Those not already washed out were encouraged to and given every opportunity to quit. Many found the training and pressure too intense and bowed out.

Those that forged ahead were now faced with the "qualification course." Here small unit tactics were taught and practiced in a three week period. More candidates were coaxed to leave the program. Those that remained were sent to Camp Mackall where specific training in hand to hand combat, survival skills, leadership and much more was taught.

The training and the quest to eliminate the weakest links continued when each candidate was sent on for specialty training in one of five areas: weapons, intelligence, medical, engineering or communications. Some courses lasted as long as 42 weeks and were followed by language training which tacked on yet another 8 to 12 weeks. The final hurdle to be cleared was the unconventional warfare exercise. Once that was completed, the Special Forces had a new Green Beret. Although officers followed a different course, it was equally challenging. Officers were being incorporated into the Special Forces but remained somewhat of a rarity. Silver wings pinned to your chest, bloused trousers and jump boots topped off with the Green Beret, your service record was only missing one thing, practical experience. No soldier in the world could claim to have trained harder or longer. The pride was unmatched.

Once graduated, a Green Beret would receive his orders that would take him to various duties. By 1967, if your orders read "MACV-SOG," you would be reporting to Military Assistance Command Vietnam, Studies and Observation Group. The last part, SOG, was the most worrisome. It was highly secretive, and word had it that working for SOG could be hazardous to your health. Word also had it that soon after reporting to SOG you would be issued a non descript black hat and denied the right to wear the Green Beret you had just worked your balls off for.

Whether William Colby coined the acronym SOG or one of his many minions did is unclear. Simply put, SOG or Studies and Observation Group, was a tool of the CIA. Funding SOG operations into Laos and Cambodia was an expensive proposition and came right out of the deep pockets of the CIA. The amalgamation of the S.F., CIA and SOG seemed to be natural and a good union.

Although S.F. had served as advisers and had trained ARVN (Army of the Republic of Vietnam) for some time, 1965 would open a new chapter. Special Forces expanded role would be shadowy and sinister, placing S.F. soldiers directly in harm's way. Many new chapters would be added to the legend of the Green Berets.

The all volunteer S.F. skimmed the" crème de la crème" from the regular Army's N.C.O. (non Commissioned Officers) corps. These Sergeants were to become the backbone for SOGs operation into Cambodia and Laos. The experience and longevity of their training virtually eliminated the imposters and even motivated individuals who had already experienced success. SOG was to receive some of the finest young men America had to offer. Lieutenant Bill Vowell, assigned to SOG's FOB1, offered this analysis of the N.C.O.'s he encountered, "The N.C.O.s were by and large top notch . . . the fatal flaw which many of them had, as I was soon to find out, was a flair for bravery which closely paralled an active death wish."

The unofficial coat of arms for SOG; officially SOG did not exist. Sketch by Star Barkman.

The methods and training S.F. practiced could never be construed as your father's Army. Completely "outside the box," S.F. was comfortable with tactics and procedures not used with line companies still being trained with World War II conventional methods. The missions into Laos and Cambodia would be lead by the most experienced and capable men available. A first lieutenant may have to place both his pride and silver bars aside until his experience caught up to his rank and education. In the world of Special Forces it was not uncommon for a graduate from the University of Illinois to listen to and take orders from an 8th grade dropout from the "Green Lawns Middle School." Operating outside of Vietnam, SOG men would be confronted with more and certainly different hurdles to clear. Like <u>Mission Impossible</u>, any of SOGs operatives discovered in Laos or Cambodia would be disavowed. The U.S. presence in Vietnam was already under scrutiny in the media, in Hollywood and on college campuses. Joe Q Public would not be privy to any ground forces operating in Laos or Cambodia, for any reason. 1965 marked the beginning of American S.F. under SOGs control. Secrecy would need to be maintained and that alone presented a very high hurdle. At first S.F. personnel would be "sanitized" while operating in the neutral countries. No dog tags, conventional weapons, U.S. uniforms and, of course, no Green Beret. In addition, should an injury or death occur, as they would, the casualty would be attributed to having occurred while operating with a conventional unit inside South Vietnam.

To further complicate SOGs missions into Vietnam's neighboring countries, the missions had to originate from an F.O.B. (forward operating base) located inside of South Vietnam's borders. The reconnaissance teams staged at the various F.O.B.s would have to be transported by helicopter and vertically inserted into the "denied areas." Once there, the RTs (recon teams) would monitor the traffic moving from the North to the South and scout and report all pertinent activity on or near the Ho Chi Minh Trail. "Snoop'n and poop'n" in Uncle Ho's neighborhood, where Ho's nephews had operated virtually unscathed, took the Communists totally by surprise. The watchful eyes of the RTs were viewed as a real threat by the NVA and from the very beginning Laos and Cambodia "would be very dangerous places to be."

A recon team would usually be lead by a S.F. senior N.C.O. or occasionally an officer, most often a first lieutenant. The leader would be given call sign 1-0 for radio communications purposes. An assistant team leader, also an N.C.O. with less experience, was given the radio call sign (1-1). The all important radio operator was assigned the 1-2 designation and the task of "humping" the PRC-25 radio, fondly renamed the "Prick 25." Battery operated, the radio added 23.5 pounds to the already burdened S.F. man who also had to carry extra batteries and additional antennae. The operator also carried his weapon, water, ammo, C-rats and more. It was a job for a man with young legs. At times additional S.F. soldiers would join the team and were referred to as "strap hangers." They went along for the purpose of gaining experience. Occasionally, a passing S.F. member would jump in to "lend a hand." The world of the Green Beret and SOG was small, and helping a friend you knew was completely acceptable. The recon teams had flexibility far beyond anything practiced in the regular Army. S.F. and SOG had developed this approach in order to survive and be successful.

To beef up and give the R.T. some physical presence the Americans contracted "Indigs," or indigenous personnel to join the team. These mercenaries were paid by SOG and were therefore employed by the CIA. In Southeast Asia the Indigs might be Chinese, Cambodian or Montanyard, depending on where the special ops took place. The number taken on a mission depended on the availability of the resource and the demands of the mission itself. Both language and cultural difference also affected the number of Indigs that could be managed successfully under circumstances that would invariably be life or death.

Each team would train themselves in weapons, stealth, explosives and conditioning. Some RT leaders were better at connecting with the Indigs than others and could expect more success on their missions and have a life expectancy that would be acceptable under very dangerous conditions. These recon teams would become the first "boots on the ground" to enter Laos under American leadership. Because of the distances, rivers, jungles and mountains, the SOG teams were inserted by helicopters from their F.O.B.s located in Vietnam just outside the Laotian border. Initially the team's goals were to simply gather intelligence on and around the Ho Chi Minh Trail in both Laos and Cambodia. However, this changed as the war ground on.

Because William Colby's earlier efforts at gathering "intel" along the trail had met with less success than desired, SOGs presence was a huge upgrade at least that is what the CIA was counting on. The question as to how many NVA were observed what weapons were being transported and how many trucks were in the convoys were simple questions; the "devil was in the details." How to get to the area of operations, remaining undetected and returning alive—those were the toughest obstacles on any mission.

The Ho Chi Minh Trail bore no resemblance to any road or highway in the United States. It was a monumental physical challenge to SOG and the NVA as well. In addition to the environmental challenges, Uncle Ho's nephews now found themselves under the watchful eye of SOG RTs. Quickly a high stakes game of cat and mouse developed. The contest would not have a viewing audience, yet the consequences would be of the most serious nature.

With each passing year, and sometimes even monthly, the NVA ramped up activity on the Trail and were also receiving professional training while their weaponry was being upgraded by both China and the U.S.S.R. SOGs recon teams were always numerically inferior and initially used their superior skills to avoid contact with the NVA and Ho's department of transportation and the North's hunting parties. It was, however, inevitable for the two combatants to collide, and although short in duration, the meetings became increasingly violent. Although neither side made the public aware, men were most certainly dying.

As the U.S. conventional forces tightened the grip on northern South Vietnam by controlling waterways and unleashing air strikes on the roadways, the Ho Chi Minh Trail became even more important to Ho's war efforts in the South. With the increased trail usage by the NVA, the need to monitor the movements increased as well. By 1967, SOG had studied and they had observed. Along the way they had expanded their playbook and the NVA felt the presence of the recon teams more with each passing month. With SOGs ratcheting up of pressure and the natural demands of the environment, the Northerners began to catch it from all angles. Bill Vowell summed up the effects of SOGs trail activity. "They were mucking up Mr. Charlie's super highway by calling in airstrikes, B-52 saturation bombing and otherwise creating havoc for the other side as they tried to move supplies south . . ."

For many of the NVA soldiers, moving down the trail was their first experience in the jungle. "The dampness, oppressive heat, and rotting vegetation combined with leaches, scorpions, centipedes, ants and other types of biting, stinging, sucking insects made the jungle most inhospitable. In addition, venomous snakes, including cobras and bamboo vipers, waited in tree branches, under logs or in the grass for their next victim." In addition to the infiltrating soldiers, civilian "porters" were impressed to move the necessities of war. At first backpacks were used, and later reinforced bicycles were employed to move hundreds of pounds of rice or war making materiel. As the war progressed, truck convoys replaced bicycles and backpacks.

Like a tiny bee sting can set a 1,000 lb horse into a bucking frenzy, SOG began to rattle the NVA all along the Truong Son Route. Snakes and insects became the least of the NVA's worries. A more proactive SOG began to set up deadly ambushes, leave toe poppers (small explosive devices) in their wake that ripped off toes and feet and occasionally grab an unsuspecting NVA for "interrogation" purposes. However, of all SOGs repertoire the ability of S.F. leaders to call in air strikes was the most devastating. By 1965 American bombers and fighters began to attack routinely . . . phantom attack aircraft swooped down to tree top level and B-52s dropped tons of bombs from altitudes so high the men on the ground were unaware of the attack until the jungle erupted around them. With the addition of the attack helicopter and the always proactive Air Force Skyraiders not to mention spookys always on the prowl, the NVA lost thousands of soldiers on the Trail.

JFK's initial support of Army Special Forces was paying back dividends to the war effort. As for the N.V.A., running into S.F. professionals could ruin their weekend or worse rearrange one's health and dental records. Uncle Ho's nephews were becoming very uncomfortable "in addition to killing or wounding many infiltrators." Survivors were feeling the effects in the morale department.

U.S. Special Forces guys Sergeant Ron Bock (L) and Lieutenant Gamble Dick socialize with their Cambodian allies. Photo courtesy of Gamble Dick.

CHAPTER 3

FLYING THE FRIENDLY SKIES

Special Forces and their unholy marriage to SOG were clearly as unconventional as the regular army was regular. Encouraging independent thinking, slipping into neutral countries, "sanitized," training with foreign weapons not to mention Sergeants leading Lieutenants was viewed as radical. When the use of foreign mercenaries became known, it was easy to understand why the regular Army community viewed Special Forces and SOG as bizarre at best. Some even used the derogatory terms "green beanies," "snake eaters," and other not so flattering terms to describe them. First Lieutenant Bill Vowell offered this description "they were a collection of drunks, swashbuckling buccaneers, little removed from active pirates and that was just the officers." Vowell himself had trained for duty with the more structured 101st Airborne Division. Being rerouted to Special Forces was like sending the Mormon Tabernacle Choir to perform with Mick Jaeger. Vowell may have found himself out of his element; however, it did qualify him as a fair and balanced source on the state of affairs at FOB #1 in Phu Bai.

Flaunting their "green beanies" and bloused trousers and hijacking highly skilled N.C.O.s away from the regulars created friction. When the "bean counters" alerted the "in box thinkers" to the funds being diverted to the FNGs (fuckin new guys) it became bewildering to the Army brass. S.F. did seem to encounter less "red tape" and promoted a rogue attitude, or maybe it was just a touch of jealousy on the Army's part.

Make no mistake about it when S.F. received their assignment to SOG the two became amalgamated and sought as much anonymity and freedom to conduct "ops" as they could get. However, the regular Army's

MAC 5 S.O.G
Forward Operating Bases (6)
1967

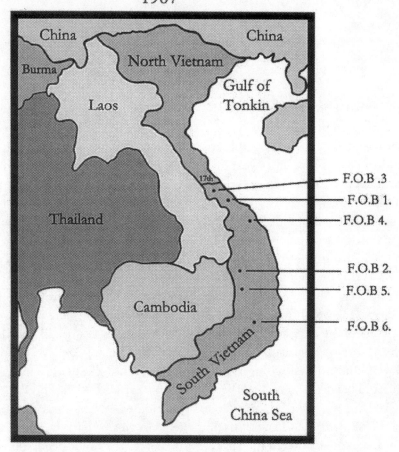

Sketch by Star Barkman.

yoke could not be completely unharnessed, S.F. operating in Laos still required support from the parent organization in the form of transportation.

SOG could not live inside Laos 24 hours a day. Laos's neutrality had to be respected; at least it must be made to appear that way. F.O.B. (forward operating bases) were established inside of South Vietnam's borders (see map) to serve as jumping off points for the RTs. Terrain dictated that the RTs would have to rely on helicopters, primarily VNAF and U.S. Army helicopters. Recon teams could not be expected to cross rivers, jungle, and mountains to "snoop and poop," and then return on foot, although it happened now and then. S.F. offered no M.O.S. (military occupational specialty) for flying helos. RTs and Hatchet Forces would have to hitch a ride with one of three sources: U.S. Army, VNAF or Marine Air Wing. There could be no mission without helos.

The cross border excursions would be known as "insertions." They would neither be simple nor safe. The insertion had to be accompanied by false insertions so the N.V.A. could be kept off balance and have to guess as to where the Recon team was actually going to deplane. Forcing the NVA to consider many L.Z.s (landing zones) was SOP and usually kept the RTs safe on their trip inbound, usually, but not always. At some point the RT had to be exfiltrated or returned. This could take place after several minutes, hours or if undetected, following several days. Exfiltration could be accomplished by having SOG teams rendezvous with a helicopter at a landing zone (L.Z.). Finding a suitable place for a helo to set down was often difficult because of trees, degree of slope, large rocks or the presence of the enemy. Smaller teams could even be exfiltrated by extending a rope with foot loops from a helo (known as a McGuire Rig) and then raising them vertically to safety. Later, the foot loops were replaced by a harness and was termed a "Stabo Rig" which featured more security.

As SOG became more of a threat to the NVA traffic on the "trail" the NVA stepped up their efforts to eliminate the RTs with added patrols, snipers, and trained tracking teams. In some places, K-9 assistance was added to the NVA arsenal in order to ferret out and kill the RTs.

SOGs stepped up "Black Ops," or dirty tricks as the enemy saw them undoubtedly provided the NVA with extra motivation to eliminate their tormentors. Snatching POWs was not common, but did occur. Planting exploding ammunition in weapons/ammo caches also qualified as hitting below the belt. One insidious little gadget was called a "nightingale device," planted inside an NVA encampment it was fitted with a timer and when the recon team was on their way the nightingale went off. It mimicked the sounds of an enemy attack and sent the sleepy camp into a panic, hopefully killing many of their own in the darkened camp. Some claim electronics were also incorporated into the N.V.A.'s tool box.

The violent fire fights that erupted pitting the RTs against the numerically superior NVA often left S.F. troopers and their mercenary comrades with serious wounds and worse. These circumstances would be cause to exfiltrate the RT. Besides encounters with the NVA, a broken ankle, snake bite, or a severe case of dysentery may also require Hueys to exfiltrate the RT from a pre-arranged PZ (pick up zone). An emergency could happen at any time, which was totally unpredictable. Helicopters had to be available 24-7. This availability of helos was known as being "dedicated."

Army pilots were generally warrant officers. This was a peculiar hybrid that loosely combined a potential officer candidate with a possible NCO to be. The position seemed to have candidates gravitate to it—unconventional types with attitudes that at least resembled those of the SF men they would be transporting. Uncle Ho's neighborhood was no friendlier in the air than it was on the ground. The connection between the helos and the tormentors they disgorged did not go unnoticed on the Ho Chi Minh Trail. No self-respecting NVA gunner could pass up an opportunity to terminate a Huey and send it crashing to the ground in a huge fireball.

The marriage between SOG and the helos furnished by the U.S. Army and the VNAF formed a blissful union. The pilots, crews, and the men from SOG were seemingly cut from the same bolt of cloth. There were no milk runs when flying into "denied" areas. Huey pilots took mega risks on a regular basis and pushed their aircraft well beyond the recommended limits. Age may have been a factor; some of the pilots were barely over 20 and believed themselves to be ten feet tall and bullet proof. There was always hope for recon teams and Hatchet Forces who found themselves in grave danger as long as they could communicate with the pilots and crews flying above them. A mutual admiration was forged from the perilous work both performed under the duress that came from the very unique situation found in Laos. Special Forces soldiers recognized the importance of the Army helo crews sometimes lead by twenty year old pilots who in turn saw the SF men as superheroes.

SOG was also fortunate to tap into an asset the U.S.A.F. began developing during WWII, the acronym FAC which stood for Forward Air Controller. FAC pilots flew prop driven light aircraft at low altitude and slow speeds which enabled the pilot to visualize battlefield conditions as well as control and tailor other air assets for the Recon teams and Hatchet Forces who so often found themselves in a jam.

FAC pilots originally flew the Cessna "01 bird dog." It was upgraded by the "02 Cessna Skymaster," which later gave way to the North American OV-10. FAC aircraft that flew into Laos were call signed "Covey" followed by a 50 series number, if the flight originated out of Khe Sanh. If flying from Da Nang, a 200 series number was assigned. As the war ground on and the North Vietnamese received sophisticated anti-aircraft equipment, primarily near Hanoi, the U.S.A.F. began using the F-100 F or "super saber" as a FAC. Flying under the call sign "Misty," the super saber was a testament to the dangerous nature of flying "FAC" missions in the prop driven aircraft.

Regardless of which type of aircraft was flown or where it originated from, FAC pilots took on a lions share of decision making along with the ever present danger of being shot down, killed or worse, captured. Misty pilots had the advantage of flying their Super Sabers at higher speeds yet still suffered 28% shoot downs in South East Asia.

FAC pilots played a huge role in America's secret war in Laos and Cambodia and brought whatever order and organization possible to the chaos on the ground. One such pilot was Air Force Captain Corwin Kippenhan who was shot out of the sky "up north," spent the night escaping and evading the North Vietnamese and was rescued the following morning. The Air Force wasted little time "rewarding" Kippenhan by sending him to train in the 02 Skymaster. After ten days or so of training, the Captain qualified and was assigned to fly missions in support of SOG ops into Laos. "Kip" Kippenhan had jumped from the frying pan directly into the fire.

The sound of the FAC's single engine alone was assurance to the Special Forces soldiers that help was only a radio call away. It should come as no surprise those NVA gunners on or near the Ho Chi Minh Trail found FAC aircraft to be a highly prized target. The NVA had connected the dots and were wise to FACs relationship with SOGs ops. Downing a FAC aircraft and sending its pilot for an extended stay at the notorious Hanoi Hilton was an NVA gunner's dream. No greater scalp could dangle from the belt of Ho Chi Minh's sharpshooters than that of an FAC pilot.

Although observation aircraft moved slowly and packed no bombs or guns it could, on its own, bring a "world of shit" crashing down on the NVA and the Trail. FAC had a deadly list of "friends" available to them, friends that could and would make any NVA run for his life.

One such asset that made its presence felt in Laos and South East Asia was the A1-E Skyraider. Like the T Rex in Jurassic Park, the Skyraider found new life in the skies over Southeast Asia. The vintage fighter bomber first appeared at the close of WW II, saw extended action in Korea, and was "moth balled" by the Air Force and the US Navy. The prop driven dinosaur made a ghostly reappearance in South East Asia when the Air Force assigned highly motivated and proactive pilots to the cockpits of the old war birds. The A1-Es took the call sign "Sandies" and flew out of U Dorn Royal Tai Air Base (RTAB) in Thailand. In action around Hill 891 in Laos, the Sandies were members of the 602nd Fighter's Squadron where they flew missions in support of the Air Force Jolly Green rescue helos. They also provided close air support for SOG and went on hunting trips along the Ho Chi Minh Trail.

The Skyraider lacked updated technology and speed, but it possessed a rare combination of capabilities that, when teamed with veteran A.F. pilots, was still deadly twenty years after it first appeared. The A1-E could loiter on station for long periods of time, possessed cannons, rockets and napalm. They were responsible for saving the lives of countless Americans in South East Asia. With the power to knock out enemy trucks, boats, and bunkers, the A1-E was a relentless attacker of NVA troops.

As for the A1-E, it was vulnerable to ground fire and lacked the speed to consistently fend off a Mig attack. Sadly, 201 Skyraiders were lost during the Vietnam War. The A1-E pilots would earn many citations for bravery as would be the case on Hill 891 in Laos.

U.S. Air Force HH-3H Jolly Green Giant Helicopter sent to rescue recon team Flatfoot on Hill 891 in Laos. Sketch by Star Barkman.

SOG's affiliation with Hueys, FACs and Skyraiders was bolstered by yet another Air Force asset known as the "Jolly Green Giant." The HH-3H helicopter was specifically designed by Sikorsky for rescue purposes. For Laotian operations, the J.G. flew out of Da Nang Air Base and was assigned to the 37th Aerospace Rescue and Recovery Squadron. The "Jolly" was manned by a four man crew that the Air Force had painstakingly trained and educated. Both officers and crew were totally committed to their rescue missions and to their fellow crew men. The aircraft was commanded by the pilot and co-pilot (officers), a flight engineer (FE), and the Pararescue man (PJ) rounded out the remainder of the crew. Jolly crews could trace their origins back to an incident in the China Burma Theatre during WW II. There being no trained rescue teams, a hastily organized group of volunteers parachuted (some without training) into a group in trouble. Despite the spontaneous nature of the rescue mission, it came off without a hitch.

The Air Force recognized the need for a professionally trained and organized rescue team, one that could succeed as a result of training should luck and fate fail. Their work in Vietnam, and especially on Hill 891 in Laos, is legendary, and their courageous work continues today in Iraq and Afghanistan.

Picking up astronauts and their capsules was once part of the JG mission. Today's JG crews have a wider variety of possibilities to train for. Although their own downed pilots are of special interest, the film <u>The Perfect Storm</u> featured a JG crew attempting a sea rescue during a hurricane. Jolly crews train for all rescue scenarios from desert to ocean and as they did in Laos, mountainous jungles. Jolly crews often crossed service lines to perform their special bravery and found any rescue, regardless of who it was for, a challenge they could not turn down.

It should come as no surprise that most Jollies were commanded by career officers who had in many cases graduated from the prestigious U.S.A.F. Academy. Many had piloted other types of aircraft previously and were very skilled aviators even before commanding Jollies. At best, rescues were dicey propositions and the aircraft commanders shouldered enormous decisions on each mission. Decisions had to be made that often placed both rescuers and their targets in peril. It was their training, education, and above all, their character that made Jolly pilots extra ordinary men and flyers. A flight engineer (FE) was essential to every crew and aircraft. Affectionately referred to as a "gam" or "greasy ass mechanic," the job was for the technically oriented. Several years were spent as an on the ground flight mechanic prior to qualifying for F.E. In addition, repair and maintenance of the aircraft's hydraulics and electronics also had to be mastered. Once in the air the FE manned one of the Jolly machine guns and also operated the powerful hoist for rescues where the helo could not land. The FE determined the "Alpha One" status of the helo which roughly translated means its readiness to fly. That judgment could determine the safety of an entire crew, including himself.

The crew had one final component, the PJ or Pararescue man. A rescue specialist, the PJ had survived 18 months of intense training in what was termed the "pipeline." The Air Force's only elite operation, they have never received the notoriety the Army Special Forces or the Navy Seals have. PJs received training in field medicine and weapons not to mention underwater ops and HALO jumps (high altitude low opening) which should not be tried at home. Prior to donning the maroon beret, all phases had to be mastered, training with anything that floats, flies or has wheels. PJs have continued to do what they do best, save lives. Most recently, PJs have found their way to both Iraq and Afghanistan and have lived up to their motto "that others may live." One hundred percent volunteers, they chose to do it in South East Asia and have continued to choose in Afghanistan. No more capable rescuers exist. The demands of the position limit the duration of a PJs career to 5 ½ years on average. Retired PJ, Wayne Fisk, once posed the question, "where do we get these brave young men from?" Where indeed?

Despite having designated Army piloted helos, SOGs demand for transportation sometimes overwhelmed the supply of helos available. To augment the transportation supply, it occasionally became necessary to request Marine helos to insert or exfiltrate SOGs, recon teams, and Hatchet Forces.

It was not as if the Marine helos were under worked. Operating in the extreme northern section of South Vietnam, Marine helos worked in and around places like Con Thien and Khe Sanh where resupply was a regular run and removing Marine casualties was also common. The Marine air crews developed a grudging respect for SOG's recon teams and Hatchet Forces, who like themselves, often defied the odds. They were men of the same ilk. Marine flyers could trace their lineage back to Major Greg "Pappy" Boyington. Some of his aviation genes had been passed along to the proud helo crews serving in South East Asia. Hundreds of Marine "grunts" still living today owe their lives to the highly professional crews that flew Marine helicopters.

SOGs transportation demands often compromised their desire to remain independent and anonymous. This was never truer than the SOGs use of the VNAF. The Vietnamese Air Force was a fledging group of flyers supplied with U.S. built helos (albeit old ones) and piloted by veteran South Vietnamese who quickly built a reputation on taking risks. Some even developed their own personal uniforms, and one flew missions resplendent in genuine western wear, right down to a ten gallon hat. The VNAF flew the old H-34 Kingbees which were hand-me-downs from the U.S. Army. They were already antiques by 1967. Often covered in hydraulic fluid, noisy and blotched with patchwork, the VNAF made them work. The Kingbees would make their presence felt on Hill 891, and they became a welcome site when the alternative was to remain on a cold and wet mountainside inside Uncle Ho's neighborhood.

One final resource that was of no small consequence to SOGs, RTs, and Hatchet Forces was the ability of the C-130 aircraft to appear in times of extreme danger. A long time performer in the U.S.A.F. fleet, the C-130 had been flown since 1951, upgraded numerous times and is still serving in Iraq and Afghanistan. Versatile, dependable, and crewed by more professional airmen, the turbo prop aircraft was dubbed "Hercules" for its lifting prowess. Flown throughout the South East Asian theatre, the C-130 could take an offensive posture entitled "hunter killer" missions, cruising above the Ho Chi Minh Trail and armed with machine guns and cannon. These "Herky Birds" targeted anything that was moving from north to south. Truck convoys were the preferred prey along with anti-aircraft guns in tow. Pilots relished the hunter killer missions as they provided an amount of flexibility to the mission not to mention the increased adrenaline flow when a target-rich environment was sighted. However, the venerable aircraft was also used as a flare ship taking the call sign "Blind Bat" or "Lamplighter," depending on where the flight originated from. Although much less glamorous than Hunter Killer missions, providing SOG with daylight at night greatly increased the RTs chances of survival. Once darkness was erased as a factor that weighed in favor of the numerically superior NVA hunting parties, American Special Forces machine gunners and riflemen were able to utilize their marksmanship and better defend themselves.

In addition to exposing the NVA to the artificial daylight, a psychological lift was provided when the noise of the powerful engines could be heard high overhead. When radio contact was established between the recon team and the aircraft, the feeling of being isolated was relieved. Regardless of the role "Hercules" took on, it was one of the great successes the Air Force could point to and justify their high budget demands.

The lonely and dangerous missions taken on by SOGs recon teams and Hatchet Forces in Laos often boiled down to the resources available to the Special Forces soldier. The Skyraiders, FACs, C-130s, Jollies, Gladiators and Spartans, along with assistance from the VNAF and Marine helos all gave SOGs teams a better chance at both success and survival.

SOG could call on some highly professional and motivated assets to contribute to their well being and aid in their mission's success. However, the very nature of working in Uncle Ho's Neighborhood was totally unpredictable, always uncomfortable and too often, deadly. No master plan or crystal ball could take into account the dozens of possible scenarios that could and would develop on any given mission. Hill 891 would test the mettle of America's finest soldiers and airmen. It put their equipment, training and communications to the ultimate test.

CHAPTER 4

JOSEPH'S SILVER WINGS

FOB #1 Phu Bai, S.V.N. 1200 hours, 7 November 1967

Recon team Flatfoot spent the early part of the afternoon preparing for the mission they had been training for; a mission that would put them in neutral Laos and in close proximity to the Ho Chi Minh Trail. Their three week training period was now reduced to only several hours to fine tune the team's plan for entering Laos. Weapons check was of paramount importance, web gear, canteens, boot laces, C-rats and even the location of ammo was examined by team leader, Master Sergeant Brue Baxter. The age old question for "ground pounders" had to be answered. What do I actually need and how much weight can be humped?

The amount of time allotted Flatfoot for training was about average for SOG's recon teams preparing to operate in the shadow of the Ho Chi Minh Trail. The team would be observing NVA activity which originated in North Vietnam with the intention of moving south and making war on their neighbors. Specifically the RT was to count how many NVA were observed, what weapons were they carrying, did they wear boots or sandals, were trucks seen and any other pertinent information.

Providing the RT found what they were looking for and returned safely, the information would be put in report form and submitted to SOG. The team leader or leaders would be sent to Saigon for debriefing by the CIA and then sent packing back to their F.O.B. In Saigon the "intel" would be added to that of other missions and some sort of pattern would emerge. Eventually some sort of finished product would worm its way through bureaucratic channels and pass in front of Bureau Chief William Colby, the mastermind of the secret war in Laos and Cambodia. Colby would then have the big picture, and U.S. strategists and tacticians could make decisions that would hopefully lead to positive results for American troops in South Vietnam. It is difficult to quantify how successfully the "intel" was used to help the troops and make the war winnable. Did the Army receive the CIA reports and if so, were they put to use? The RT missions were highly problematic. The risks taken with men's lives had to be justified by someone. Were we saving more by losing some? Obviously someone felt SOGs operations were paying dividends and the ops continued past 1970.

Colby's secret war was already two years old when team Flatfoot prepared for yet another incursion into Laos. Men, almost entirely composed of Special Forces, had little time to question their own work. They were, after all, professionals who volunteered and chose their career paths. Besides, those not in the performance and survival mode wouldn't last long. Missions required every ounce of training and focus that the Special Forces men could muster.

Flatfoot would be composed of four Special Forces professionals and augmented with nine "Nungs," native soldiers trained by Special Forces. The number in Flatfoot's contingent was considered larger than most. Going into Laos "heavy" indicated that encountering more bad guys than normal may be expected.

The leadership for recon team Flatfoot would be provided by Special Forces Master Sergeant Bruce Baxter. Baxter had accrued nearly five years in Vietnam; three of those had been spent with SOG. His survival alone was testament to his expertise in Special Forces' methods. The Master Sergeant himself would personally take responsibility for schooling his recon team. It was fortuitous for all the team members to receive training from Baxter, given his experience and success. By all accounts, the Master Sergeant was a pro's pro in the ways of recon.

The three weeks of training time allotted to Baxter for training was considered about average, certainly it was not too much. Nine of the thirteen team members were "Nungs" or transplanted Chinese living in Vietnam. Chinese were not able to receive education in Vietnam, where racism was alive and well. The communication problems between the team leaders and the Nungs was a huge hurdle and cultural problems contributed mightily. Bruce Baxter had successfully trained Indigs in the past in all the necessary phases such as weapons, marksmanship, maintenance, and safety, physical fitness, and hygiene.

The mountainous jungle in Laos offered heat, humidity and elevation that affected all the team members. It seemed that no matter where you walked, the jungle offered vines, branches, and tall grasses that seemed to sprout hands with the sole purpose of exhausting every living creature that moved through them.

Baxter also had to teach the Nungs how to field strip an M-1 carbine and convey the importance of stealth and the exact meaning of hand signals. Embarking and disembarking helicopters had to be taught, along with the proper use of ambushes, the training list went on and on.

The Indigs were not afraid of soldiering, and they especially liked firing their weapons. Teaching them when to fire was a difficult concept to instruct. Bruce Baxter truly had his work cut out for him as did all the recon team leaders. Failure to integrate and train the Nungs properly was a recipe for disaster. There was a mountain of teaching and instruction but Laos was not a classroom. Here success was measured in life or death. There would be no retests.

Three Americans joined Baxter's team: Lt. Chips Fleming, Sergeant Joseph Kussick and Staff Sergeant Homer Wilson. In Vietnam, those without experience or just entering the country were referred to as "newbies." Fleming categorized himself and Wilson with the "newbie" tag. He also characterized their participation on Flatfoot as "strap hangers" or along for the ride and experience.

Fleming had spent only hours at FOB1 when he was introduced to Bruce Baxter. Baxter wasted no time and quickly requested Lt. Fleming to accompany him to Phu Bai the following day. Fleming agreed. Early the following morning Fleming sought out Baxter and the two headed for Phu Bai. Baxter had yet to explain why the trip was necessary. Their jeep bounced along the dirt roads until it pulled up to a block building with the word "Mortuary" stenciled in flat black paint just above the door.

As it turned out Baxter had made this trip before, and the "mission" was to help the mortuary staff prepare the bodies of American service men returning to their loved ones back home. Why Lt. Fleming was brought along was never made clear, although Baxter was known to be both a religious and spiritual man. He often included other Special Forces members during religious ceremonies as was the case with Lt. Dick.

If Baxter's plan was to impress upon Fleming the seriousness of their profession it was unnecessary. Fleming had spent six years with the Marines as an enlisted man. He was far from a wide-eyed cowboy type. He was already tuned in to the possibilities that lay ahead. Fleming's father served as Assistant Chief of Naval Operations, Special Operations Counter Insurgency. Alan Fleming had a good idea about what he had gotten himself into. It must have been agonizing knowing your son was constantly in harms way yet unable to communicate about it, even to the mother of your son.

Nevertheless, the three Americans were Special Forces trained volunteers and had the luxury of being able to lean heavily on Baxter's lengthy experience in Laotian operations.

Joseph Kussick was from a long line of Pennsylvanians to take up arms on behalf of his country. Just as proud as the Civil War "Buck Tails" were of their special designation, Kussick was acutely aware of his success with the Special Forces. His silver wings, jump boots and especially his green beret were worn with extra ordinary pride. He had become an elite warrior. But long before his extraordinary Green Beret experience he had achieved elite family member status. Both younger brothers Bill and Tom were the recipients of Joseph's coaching and mentoring. "It was like having two fathers." What could be better?

Joseph Kussick would be designated the "1-2" for recon team Flatfoot. He would carry the added burden of the PRC-25 radio on his back. To those who labored beneath its weight, it became known as the "Prick 25." The radio would be the sole link Flatfoot had to their covey flier, helicopters, and their forward operating base at Phu Bai. It was the single most important piece of equipment carried into the field by any recon team entering Laos or Cambodia.

Silver wings indicated the Special Forces soldier had successfully completed parachute training. Sketch by Star Barkman.

Master Sergeant Baxter quickly recognized Kussick's aptitude and talent. He immediately began to impart his own experience and training on Joseph. Kussick had heard all the stories and saw the respect Baxter received at Phu Bai. Bruce Baxter quickly took young Kussick under his wing and began instructing and mentoring him in the ways of reconnaissance. In Kussick, Baxter saw the potential for a fine Special Forces soldier. Risk taking and cowboy antics were not high on the Master Sergeant's list of positive traits for a serious Special Forces man. Joseph Kussick was ahead of his time in the maturity category and also carried a moral sense about him. He had obviously come from good stock and his family was responsible for raising a young man with a straight backbone. A mutual admiration was forged.

Perhaps Baxter's greatest challenge in training the Nungs was the weapons portion. Inattention or cheating the time allotted could get one killed even before the mission had started. The rifle most used by U.S. forces in Vietnam, the M-16, was difficult to maintain and train with. It also could not be used in neutral Laos. Lt. Chips Fleming recalled some of Flatfoot's weaponry. "We carried an odd assortment of weapons. I had a "sterile" Swedish K sub machine gun." ". . . I think some of the Indigs were carrying M-1 carbines." The M-1 was World War II vintage and had been distributed throughout the world since the 1940s making it untraceable to the U.S. At .30 caliber, the M-1 could not be considered a combat heavyweight in terms of knockdown power. However, it was training friendly, easily maintained and dependable. Guns and Ammo magazine called it "simple and rugged." In short, the rifle was a pretty good match for the Nungs and they trained rather well with it.

R.T. Flatfoot also packed in toe poppers that could be left in their wake to discourage N.V.A. trackers. Toe poppers were designed to maim an unfortunate enemy and relieve him of his foot or a large portion of it. Some Special Forces men were reluctant to utilize the insidious little device lest one of their own became confused and ended up a casualty of "friendly fire." There was no question Flatfoot deployed toe poppers during their mission to Hill 891 and their effectiveness also became very clear.

For their night defense, Flatfoot carried in an ample amount of Claymore mines, encased in plastic and propelled by a shaped charge the weapon sent out 700 one eighth inch steel balls. Effective out to fifty yards, the projectiles could be sent towards the enemy either manually or electronically. So effective, Claymores were used in Iraq and are currently in service in Afghanistan. Should the NVA close to within throwing distance, they could be greeted with M-26 grenades. Slightly smaller than a baseball, the damage caused by the steel fragments could be horrific. Recon teams would use the grenades only in a last ditch survival scenario, an unpleasant thought that had to be considered.

Colored smoke grenades were also issued for the purposes of marking the recon team's position. Popping a smoke grenade would allow aircraft to identify the RT and drop their ordnance on the bad guys. Smoke could also help locate an RT for exfiltration.

Lt. Fleming also recalled all four Americans being issued a URC-10 survival radio to add to their already heavy load. As has been the case with soldiers for centuries, each Special Forces man customized his pack and weapon to suit his personal needs and preferences.

FOB #1 Phu Bai, S.V.N. 1600 hours 7 November 1967

By 1600 hours, recon team Flatfoot was airborne, destination neutral Laos and nearly 15 miles inside of denied territory. Transportation for Flatfoot's mission was provided by the Vietnamese Air Force and their rickety old H-34 "Kingbees." Keeping a lid on these insertions was of paramount importance. A leak could spell disaster for an entire recon team and quite possibly the helicopters and crews as well.

To confuse the enemy near the Ho Chi Minh Trail, the Kingbees followed procedure by making several false insertions. "I think we actually exited the aircraft on the third insertion," recalled Chips Fleming. The recon teams exited the only door the old H-34 provided. The Kingbees were far from stealthy with a high profile design and packing a 9 cylinder engine. Fuel economy was not a priority. In 1967 however "you could blow cylinders out of it and still get yourself home."

There were a limited number of landing zones and all were treacherous places for recon teams and helos alike. Once on the ground, recon team Flatfoot wasted no time hanging around the landing zone. Baxter's recon team skillfully melted into the surrounding foliage and trees lest they get caught by a superior enemy force or come under a pre-registered mortar attack by an NVA patrol. So vulnerable were landing zones that some missions ended there even before they started.

Leaving a trail of dust, foliage, and debris in their wake, the VNAF Kingbees lifted off without incident and in trail formation slowly disappeared into the Laotian skyline heading east, back to the relative safety of South Vietnam. Now the only connection to FOB #1 or assisting aircraft would be through the PRC-25 (Prick 25) perched high on Joseph Kussick's back. Loneliness could not be allowed to dominate the thoughts of the recon team. The most immediate task at hand was to find a RON (remain overnight) position. Whatever daylight that remained had to be used wisely. The RON site had to be defendable, away from the trails, with elevation if possible, and adequately camouflaged. The RON could not be identified in total darkness. It was imperative to make a wise selection in the light of day.

Prior to locating their RON position, Baxter halted Flatfoot's movement so they could eat, listen, and watch. The meal was cold C-Rats or at least parts of C-Rats depending on the taste of each team member. A direct descendant of K-Rats (Korean War vintage), C-Rats main course was canned and could be anything from ham and limas (a.k.a. beans and mother fuckers) to pork in gravy or spaghetti and meatballs. Sometimes crackers and jelly were included, fruit cake, a tin of peanut butter or even a chocolate disc. To assist in bowel movements, canned fruit was included which could be pears, fruit cocktail (a favorite), peaches, or apple sauce.

Some guys threw everything out except the fruit, but seldom did anyone discard the thick brown plastic bag that accompanied each meal. Inside the bag was gum, toothpicks, waterproof matches sugar, salt, pepper, coffee, hot chocolate mix and the all important toilet paper. There never seemed to be enough of that. It was thin and excruciatingly abrasive. The entire deal came in a box slightly larger than a 3 x 5 file card box. Periodically, a can opener would be issued and carried on a dog tag chain. Blue heat tabs would also be drawn to warm the rations that could also be eaten cold if time or light was a factor.

After many stops to take compass readings and to listen, Master Sergeant Baxter eyed a good looking spot for an RON. Lt. "Chips" Fleming recalled the movement from the landing zone to the RON position. "I had to pee about every five minutes. Every time we stopped to listen and take our bearings I had to drain my lizard, pretty embarrassing huh?" Recon team Flatfoot had painstakingly maneuvered itself without as much as a whisper to an acceptable place to stay overnight. All their stealth and self discipline, unlike in training, now became life and death issues. "Flatfoot was now deep in Uncle Ho's neighborhood."

Sitting in a 360º configuration was the preferred positioning for teams at night. Setting their gear inside the circle, the men went about setting up their Claymore mines and toe poppers. Both were deployed facing the direction an NVA assault might come from. The Claymores were slightly convex in shape and could be set up even in the dark with their business end pointing outward. In the early morning the mines could be disarmed and retrieved for use on the next RON.

Nights spent in Laos by recon teams were endured as best as could be expected. Often cold and wet, it was eight hours of trying to remain quiet and keep a lid on your imagination and the desire to cough, sneeze or clear your throat.

The night of November 8, 1967 was particularly quiet. Sometime around 2300 hours, 11:00 p.m. civilian time (participants have conflicting memories as to the exact time), Lieutenant Fleming recalls "hearing movement off in the distance." Being located in mountainous jungle, it was presumed the noises were that of nocturnal animals or maybe just the fertile imagination of the recon team's "newbies." Nevertheless, hands tightened on rifle stocks until each knuckle took a whitish tone, sphincters quickly imitated the same effect hands were having. Each team member fought to control his urge to take a deep breath or clear his throat. When the noise faded out, everyone released the death grips they had on their weapon. But the reprieve was short lived and the noise began anew sending the recon team back into their spasms all over again. The sequence repeated several times until even the FNGs (fucking new guys) realized the noise was that of an animal, one of the two legged variety. The noise became more distinct and constant, and it moved methodically and directly towards the recon team.

Any novice camper knows how difficult it is to move around the woods or even around a campsite in total darkness. It is not possible for even a solitary hunter to move quietly at night, unable to see vines, limbs, rocks or depressions. Coughing, sneezing, tripping, or hitting your rifle barrel on a tree trunk are all distinct possibilities at night. Even the air movement can pick up body odors and betray a team's position. American diets based on beef and Asian diets based on fish could tip off an experienced nose regardless of whose face it was on.

Like a wild pheasant, Flatfoot's only hope was to remain hunkered down and react only if discovered. If this noise was an NVA patrol, they might change course or even walk past Flatfoot's position. But the NVA hunting party continued straight for Flatfoot's position as if they knew the exact path Baxter had guided his men on. Although the NVA seemed to know the precise direction to take it became equally clear they did not know the location of the RON (remain over night) position. Within minutes the hunters walked right into the RON.

The dark, quiet night suddenly erupted with small arms fire, chaos took over the night. AK-47s with their trademark stacotic bursts and green tracer rounds found their way into Flatfoot's position. The mercenaries answered back with their M-1 carbines soon to be followed by the Americans with the Swedish Ks. Their position so thoroughly exposed, Baxter ordered the Claymore mines be detonated to prevent their position from being overrun. Touching off the Claymores sent thousands of steel balls hurtling into the NVA pursuers. Howls of pain could be heard outside Flatfoot's defensive perimeter. The Claymores had stopped the NVA in their tracks and driven them backwards. The shocking power of the blasts had saved the recon team and forced the NVA to back off.

Who initiated the fire fight? Lt. Chips Fleming struggled to recall, "To tell the truth I'm not sure who opened fire first, us or them." The fog of battle had blown in. A brief lull preceded another attack on Flatfoot, but this time the NVA utilized RPGs (rocket propelled grenades). Sparks illuminated the night and deadly shrapnel flew over and through the RT's position. The explosion from the RPGs created temporary night vision blindness to the recon team's eyes. But more importantly, the use of rocket propelled grenades signaled the presence of a serious and well trained hunter, determined to kill each and every one of Baxter's team. Several times the exchange of gunfire would cease only to be followed by a rejuvenated NVA attack each seemingly to gain momentum.

Fighting for their very existence, Flatfoot met the NVA with disciplined and well placed fire. Baxter's training methods were paying dividends. What seemed like an eternity to the combatants probably lasted for less than an hour. Lt. Fleming raised the possibility of mortars being used against the recon team, making the hour of combat even more potentially lethal for Flatfoot. The introduction of mortars would indicate a very well prepared NVA, an NVA that expected company and carried a full compliment of weaponry. Although the NVA were good at ferreting out small recon teams, on this occasion, they seemed to be better than usual.

The NVA's persistence and accurate fire didn't go unnoticed by Master Sergeant Bruce Baxter. The distinct possibility of being overrun and decimated by a superior force quickly registered with the veteran SOG man. Baxter's assessment of Flatfoot's situation necessitated his requesting a "Prairie Fire Emergency." Using Joseph Kussick's radio (PRC-25), Baxter also requested an immediate extraction.

Requesting a "Prairie Fire Emergency" indicated that a very serious scenario had developed. Making the request would send every available air asset to Flatfoot's position. Pilots from any of the services would pull out all the stops regardless of what aircraft they were flying to help fellow Americans in deep trouble. Baxter's request for an extraction was aimed primarily at FOB #1, and those helicopters that ordinarily provided transportation for the recon teams working out of Phu Bai. An extraction could be requested from the U.S. Army helos of the 190th assault squadron, the South Vietnamese Air Force out of Da Nang, Marine air wing helos out of Phu Bai or U.S.A.F. rescue helos also out of Da Nang.

Recon team Flatfoot had been inserted under the watchful eyes of a Covey FAC flying out of Da Nang, South Vietnam. The slow moving O-2 observation aircraft was piloted by Air Force Captain Corwin 'Kip' Kippenhan. This was not the pilot's first rodeo. He had followed Flatfoot's insertion as he had many other recon teams' incursions into Laos. Kippenhan did not report any reason to believe Flatfoot's mission had been compromised during the insertion. Lt. Chips Fleming concurred with Kippenhan's assessment of Flatfoot's uneventful insertion and added that the movement to the RON was conducted with caution and professionalism. Although filled with apprehension and nerves this was to be expected.

How then did the NVA detect Flatfoot's presence in Laos? If the NVA had staked out Flatfoot's landing zone why didn't they engage the recon team on the landing zone? The Kingbees would have been an added bonus. Together they presented a worthy and vulnerable target. The only negative involved in engaging on the landing zone would be Flatfoot's ability to call in attack aircraft.

Perhaps the NVA preferred to utilize total darkness before launching an assault, believing darkness would favor a successful attack. Tracking the recon team at night or even following one in fading daylight would be a monumental task even for a seasoned hunting party. It was already known that the NVA utilized dogs for tracking purposes, yet Flatfoot never reported anything that alluded to the use of K-9s. It should be noted that not all tracking dogs "sound off" while trailing.

Maybe a chance encounter placed the forces on a collision course based on luck or a lack thereof. However, Lt. Fleming's description of the NVAs approach to Flatfoot's position seemed to indicate a methodical search which would rule out luck as a factor. Something as simple as a light or sound from Flatfoot's RON could have tipped off a passing patrol. The commotion the helicopters made may have grabbed the attention of an NVA troop movement. One final possibility, could the NVA monitor radio transmissions or somehow found Flatfoot's position through electronic means? There probably will never be a definitive answer as to how Flatfoot's RON was discovered. Clandestine activity such as SOG missions always seemed to be subject to cloak and dagger speculation.

Prior to Baxter's Prairie Fire Emergency request Fac pilot Kippenhan had requested the immediate exfiltration of Flatfoot, stating that the team had been compromised. Kippenhan was shocked when his radio came to life and the sender clearly stated ". . . negative on the exfiltration. Flatfoot is to stay and accomplish as much as possible." Kippenhan returned to the radio relaying a report that Sergeant Baxter had been blinded, whether it was night blindness or an actual injury was unclear.

Kippenhan's fuel gauge now dictated he return to Phu Bai for a fill up. In Air Force lingo, he was "bingo" on fuel. "Accomplish as much as possible?" Kippenhan could not clear his mind of the decision to leave the recon team on Hill 891. The time to exfiltrate had passed. As he brought his aircraft to a halt near the fueling area, the Captain quickly made his way to the "shitter," his bowels now dictated priority. He then moved on to the Tactical Operations Center. Having flown for over 5 hours in the cramped O-2 cockpit, he assumed some down time would be in order. Instead he was told that Recon Team Flatfoot was in serious trouble and had to be exfiltrated. "As if this was news to me" was Kippenhan's response.

Corwin Kippenhan had developed an admiration for the Army Special Forces and especially for SOG teams that often (too often in Kippenhan's estimation) found themselves in serious jeopardy. In short, the Air Force Captain had a conscience and it troubled him deeply to observe the SOG men killed and maimed at an alarming rate.

Why was there a delay in the exfiltration of recon team Flatfoot? The highly experienced Bruce Baxter had declared a Prairie Fire Emergency and questioning his judgment seems incomprehensible. Captain Corwin Kippenhan piloted the O-2 Cessna and had clearly requested Flatfoot's exfiltration. Did someone at FOB Phu Bai feel threatened by the request from an Air Force Captain? There was not time for a debate and Kippenhan quickly found himself climbing aboard his O-2 for a curtain call over Hill 891. At least on this trip Kip would not be alone. Special Forces Sergeant Dudley Nutter had been assigned to the O-2s right seat. The position was known as a "Covey Rider." Nutter was there to assist the pilot in unraveling Flatfoot's predicament.

Nutter and Kippenhan had worked together before. Now they were paired again and ordered to Hill 891 to help make sense of the developing disaster that was already out of hand. Bumping down the primitive runway, both pilot and rider were acutely aware they were flying directly towards trouble. Not twenty minutes into the flight, Sergeant Nutter's voice came over the pilot's headset. "We just got hosed down by a .50 caliber machine gun." The NVA machine gun had plenty of juice to terminate the slow moving Cessna's flight and send both Kippenhan and Nutter to an early demise or worse, an all expenses paid trip to the Hanoi Hilton. Only weeks before Kippenhan's F-100 Misty Fac had been shot down within sight of Hanoi city lights. He spent the night escaping and evading and was rescued at first light. As one would expect, the event made an impression on the Air Force Academy graduate.

Neither the Cessna nor the occupants had been hit, but the incident served as a reminder that when flying in the vicinity of the "Trail" there was no way to hide. Whether it was the stressful situation or the Phu Bai chow, Kippenhan's digestive system continued to bark at him. Despite the ground fire and gas pains the O-2 continued on towards Bruce Baxter's besieged recon team. After 10 minutes or so the observation aircraft passed over and slightly to the front of Flatfoot's position on Hill 891. Nutter strained to catch a glimpse of the exchange of fire going on below. Kippenhan circled and flew figure eights while listening to any radio traffic that might help understand the situation below.

Not only had the situation not improved, it had actually deteriorated and the volume of enemy fire had increased along with reports of the enemy employing rocket propelled grenades and mortars. Recon team Flatfoot was hanging on, but just barely. Kippenhan was not shocked by the situation below, but he was appalled that the recon team had not been rescued when first compromised. Quickly he got on his radio and sent a message to Da Nang requesting an Air Force helo be sent ASAP. Remaining within his own service, Kip's request was immediately granted and two Jolly Green HH-3s were readied to perform their specialty, saving lives. Kippenhan wondered if it wasn't already too late.

With radio traffic on the increase and the recon team's survival in serious jeopardy, word was beginning to spread throughout the SOG community. Two VNAF Kingbee helicopters operating near Hill 891 and heading back to Da Nang heard of Flatfoot's predicament and immediately flew to the team's position. Kingbee pilots had built a well deserved reputation for their aviation skills, their penance for risking their lives, and proving their worthiness. The combination of characteristics they had developed fit SOG's operation to a tee and had saved the lives of many recon teams and Hatchet Forces in peril. A few of the pilots had even flown for the French and were serious aviators committed to keeping South Vietnam independent.

True to their gambling reputations, one of the ancient Kingbees suddenly swooped down to the mountainside and hovered near Flatfoot's position. Flatfoot's team members were astonished and relieved to see the possibility of escape show up as if sent from heaven. The presence of the Kingbee was obviously viewed in a different light by the NVA. The AK-47 fire picked up in volume now targeting the dilapidated old helo. Green tracers streaked across no man's land, relieving pressure on the beleaguered recon team if only temporarily. The Kingbee pilot seemed totally unphased by the angry reception he and his aircraft received. Master Sergeant Bruce Baxter read the situation perfectly ordering Wilson and Lt. Chips Fleming to gather four of their Nungs and "get the hell out of here." There was no need to repeat the order. Even strap hangers understood the situation for what it was, dire! No one seemed to mind that they were boarding an antique helicopter piloted by someone who spoke little English and had received very little formal training. The old H-34 vibrated and shook as the VNAF pilot coaxed his aircraft off the ground. Ever so slowly the Kingbee gained altitude, cleared the area, and turned east toward Phu Bai. How frustrating it must have been for the NVA to have watched their prey, or at least some of them, be whisked away just when their annihilation seemed certain.

Fleming had received shrapnel wounds to his back which likely resulted from RPG fire. To this day shrapnel occasionally works its way to the surface of his back and is removed at home. He was awarded a Purple Heart for his wounds and later received the CIB (Combat Infantry Badge) for his participation in the fire fight. This would not be the last action Fleming would see in Laos. He was treated, observed overnight, and released from Hue Phu Bai Hospital the morning of November 9th. That same morning Wilson and Fleming were hustled off to Saigon for debriefing. The two strap hangers were still in shock when they were interviewed by two men, one a regular Army officer, the other a sketchy character presumably a CIA "spook." The interrogators seemed to be both dismissive and disinterested. Perhaps they were missing their tennis match or an appointment with one of Saigon's many "boom boom" girls.

Both Wilson and Fleming were new to the reconnaissance business and had been in survival mode. Details were not their primary interest on Hill 891. The main gist of their report was that "there were a lot of bad men out there and they were attempting to kill us." It wasn't long before the interrogators grew frustrated and they abruptly dismissed the SOG men. Neither could recall the use of water boarding techniques and soon they were heading back to FOB #1 Phu Bai without being afforded the opportunity to sample any of Saigon's recreational activities.

While Fleming, Wilson and four Nungs had been saved by the first Kingbee helicopter, the remainder of the recon team held on in anticipation of the second. Baxter, Kussick and the Nungs stubbornly held their position but found themselves in a world of shit. Half the team had been safely exfiltrated but their absence left Flatfoot with only half the fire power to hold off the NVA hunting party which seemed to be growing in numbers and ferocity.

The second Kingbee pilot was no more impressed with the NVA marksmanship than was the first, and his helo also abruptly dipped from the sky and also went into a hover not far from Baxter and Kussick's position. By now the NVA had adjusted their weapons and reloaded. Clearly frustrated by watching half their quarries disappear from beneath their noses, they were ready and waiting for Kingbee #2.

The old H-34 presented a high silhouette and moved at tortoise like speeds. It gained the unwanted attention of each and every NVA soldier on Hill 891. Now completely "sighted in," Uncle Ho's hunters unleashed a furious salvo at the courageous SVN pilot and his crew. Tough as it was, the vintage aircraft began to spew wisps of smoke and it shuddered and moved in spurts and halts. The Kingbee had lost its hydraulic system and quite possibly had several cylinders shot out. The pilot could not continue to hover and began to move out of the kill zone. His helo limped and coughed like a TB patient. The remainder of the Recon Team could not climb aboard. Their hearts must have sunk as they watched the Kingbee sputter its way out of sight.

It was later learned that Kingbee #2 never made it out of Laos, crash landing in the jungle three miles from Hill 891, 45 kilometers east southeast of Muang Nong and 5 kilometers southwest of Aching, Salavan Province, Laos. In a fortuitous twist of fate neither the pilot nor crew were injured seriously. After a very scary night they were all rescued the following morning, although the venerable old Kingbee had flown its last mission.

CHAPTER 5

GOOD PILOTS TOO

Hill 891 Laos, 2100 hours, 8 November 1967

The O-2 Cessna continued to loiter above Baxter's battered and depleted recon team waiting for more rescuers and continually assuring Joseph Kussick that help was just over the next mountain. As promised, 4 U.S. Army Huey helicopters roared onto the scene and quickly made radio contact with Covey 57, which had replaced Corwin Kippenhan's Cessna.

Unlike the old H-34 Kingbees, the Huey had a new low profile design with doors on both sides. Some were outfitted specifically for assault (gunships) and some for transport (slicks). Although pilots reported a lack of power, the Huey became the most lasting image of the Vietnam War. American ground troops viewed the Huey as their life line to safety and superior medical treatment.

The U.S. Army had their own flight school for their helo pilots. Unlike the Air Force, Army pilots were not true officers but warrant officers; a curious hybrid cross of part non-commissioned officer and officer. Many of the Army pilots were barely over 20 years old and quickly gained a reputation for their willingness to take risks and gambles on behalf of the ground pounders they flew in and out of danger. Such was certainly the case with the crews of the 2 UH-1D slicks and the 2 UH-1C gun ships sent to rescue recon team Flatfoot courtesy of the 190th (A.H.C.) Attack Helicopter Company.

The crews contributed to their own growing legend and fame by painting serpents, dragons, and scantily clad girlfriends on the nose of their helicopters, a legacy bequeathed from World War II aviators.

Like a teenager with a borrowed Corvette the youthful pilots could yes sir superiors to death then disappear out of sight and do as they damn well pleased. In his book Firebirds, Chuck Carlock described pilots as "independent types who approached careers and lives in a cavalier manner."

The remnants of recon team Flatfoot would now have to rely on the Bell Company made Hueys and the skill and cavalier attitude of Warrant Officer Ira Taylor's two crews. The Army helos had been dispatched from Hue City. They were part of the 190th Assault Helicopter Company, 145th Aviation Battalion, and 12th Aviation Group. Warrant Officer Ralph Williams was paired with Ira Taylor and took the lead. Warrant Officers Kent Woolridge and William Zanow followed in trail formation. Zanow recalled the details they received at their mission briefing: they were to fly 75 miles west to a remote mountainous area in Laos, extract a Special Forces recon team at night from a mountainous jungle site. The recon team was currently engaged with the enemy. Zanow also recalled the feelings of the pilots. The mission had all the necessary ingredients present for a recipe for disaster.

The pilot's feelings notwithstanding, the two Huey Slicks were airborne shortly after 22:30 hours for what would be nearly an hour flight to Hill 891 where Woolridge and Zanow would be greeted by more chaos than either could possibly imagine.

Neither Taylor's or Wooldridge's ships reported anything out of the ordinary during their one hour flight to the mountainside which raised the crew's hopes that the mission would go better than originally expected, however, the situation on Hill 891 continued to worsen. Baxter, Kussick and the remaining Nungs clung stubbornly to the side of Hill 891. Flatfoot remained fully engaged with the NVA whose numbers seemed to grow with each passing hour. Baxter's team was managing to stalemate the NVA; however, the possibility of being overrun and annihilated was on everyone's mind. So close to Flatfoot's position were the NVA that Master Sergeant Baxter was whispering into the radio microphone and explosions and small arms fire could be heard through their radios by numerous aircraft over the scene.

The Huey helicopter became the lifeline to Americans in Southeast Asia.
Sketch by Star Barkman

Two Huey gunships had also arrived over Hill 891, in response to Flatfoot's predicament. Covey 57 (now the forward air controller) had them line up for a firing run. Warrant Officer Don Monk was the commander of the lead Gladiator and the right seat was filled by Warrant Officer Cletus Farmer. Just before the firing runs could be initiated two Air Force A1-E Skyraiders appeared over Hill 891 and with the C-130 flare ship circling high above, Hill 891 became reminiscent of Newark International Airport the day before Thanksgiving.

Communication between aircraft and from ground units to aircraft now took on the significance of life and death status. Every action taken by aircraft affected those on the ground and the other aircraft operating high above. The fact that the U.S. Army, U.S. Air Force, and the Vietnamese Air Force all were deeply involved contributed to the chaos.

The radios were full of reports, requests, and orders that at times became a jigsaw puzzle, not with pieces but with words. (Although not as chaotic to the military readers, you may want to use the following list to untangle the call signs each aircraft and ground unit used. The parent unit had assigned a name or call sign to each aircraft and ground participant for identification purposes while using the radio).

Flatfoot—original SOG team inserted on Hill 891
Bulldog—the hatchet force inserted to rescue Flatfoot
Jolly Green or J.G.—US Air Force rescue helos (2) #26 and #29
Sandies—US Air Force fighter bombers (4)
Gladiators—Army attack helos (2)
Spartan—Army transport helos (2)
Kingbees—VNAF helos (at least 2)
Covey—US Air Force Cessna 02 forward air controller (2)
Blind Bat—US Air Force C-130 flare ship (1)
Lamplighter—US Air Force C-130 flare ship (1)
Alley Cat—night time airborne command and control aircraft C-130
Crown—rescue control aircraft US Air Force C-130
Hillsboro—daytime airborne command US Air Force C-130
Queen—search and rescue center Tan Son Nhut air base

The weight of controlling the aircraft fell on the considerable shoulders of the forward air controller, Covey 57. He alone had to keep his assets from tangling into each other, a daunting task. There was one thing that was clear, with fuel running low, the Army attack helos had to be unleashed immediately and they were. Monk and Farmer's assault helo cruised across the face of Hill 891, passing the recon team's position, while spewing a deadly cocktail of 2.75 rockets, 40 millimeter belt fed grenades, and a steady diet of mini gun fire. The NVA were now getting an ass kicking from the gunships. Each firing run made by the Gladiators was answered with AK-47 fire and machine guns. Green tracers were clearly visible and came from numerous places on the side of the mountain. While the gunships softened up the side of Hill 891, the two rescue ships circled waiting their turn to ply their skills.

Taylor and Woolridge noted the attention the Gladiators received and realized how difficult their job was going to be. William Zanow recalled his thoughts while circling 7,500 feet above ground level. "I well remember the three persistent concerns I had while we were circling the area awaiting clearance to land; first and foremost I was afraid the Air Force flair ship (C-130) flying well above our altitude might unknowingly drop a flair above us and prior to reaching its predetermined illumination level it might tangle in our rotor system. My second concern was that we did not have a lot of reserve fuel remaining and if they (Covey 57) kept us in the holding pattern much longer we would not be able to complete the mission and still have sufficient fuel to return to our base camp. And finally it was freezing cold at higher altitudes . . ." Hueys were notoriously under-powered and the heater, if left on, might affect a takeoff with the remaining recon team aboard. This may not have been <u>Mission Impossible</u>, but Zanow sensed all the negative possibilities. Forebodings or not, the two rescue ships were committed and would not waste the assault helos work; the die had been cast for the Army helos.

Pilot Kent Woolridge recalled the night as "particularly dark" which made Covey 57's job of juggling all the aircraft a dangerous proposition. With 4 Army Hueys, 2 Air Force A1-Es, an Air Force C-130, 57's own Cessna and an occasional Vietnamese Air Force helo, the traffic and darkness put all participants at risk.

To minimize the effects of the super dark night, Covey 57 called on the Air Force C-130 flare ship call sign "Blind Bat 03" to turn darkness into light. As one C-130 radio man once bragged, "We can provide enough light so you can read the fine print on your divorce papers." The flares they dropped were attached to parachutes. They helped clear the fog of war and provided psychological comfort to the recon team below.

While the overall effect was positive, the descending light was annoying and at times disoriented the pilot's eyes. Zanow's fear of the parachute becoming entangled in the rotors was also a legitimate concern.

The assault helicopter piloted by Don Monk and Cletus Farmer continued to strafe suspected NVA positions. The two pilots shared the duties of firing their primary weapons. Farmer controlled the mini-guns while Monk fired the rockets. The mini-guns were powered by electricity and were a wood pile cousin of the U.S. Calvary's Gatling guns dating all the way back to General George A. Custer and the Indian Wars. Fortunately, the updated mini-gun could crank out 2,000 rounds per minute with every 7th round being a tracer. This allowed the gunner to work a stream of lethal bullets into the enemy's' positions. Farmer recalled: "We could see the green North Vietnamese tracers and muzzle flashes and I worked a steady stream of mini gun tracers among them." It was clear to Farmer that his fire was killing dozens of them.

Yet after each run a calm, clear, voice came up on each of the aircraft's radios. It belonged to Master Sergeant Bruce Baxter and each time he reported his recon team was still under heavy fire. His reports raised two questions: one, How many North Vietnamese were on Hill 891? And, how could Bruce Baxter remain such a professional under the most dire conditions?

If the rocket fire and mini-guns from the Gladiator weren't creating enough sound and fury, two Air Force A1-E Skyraiders began to pound the outlying areas around Hill 891. The venerable old prop driven aircraft were led in by Major Jimmy Kilbourne along with his wingman, Major Robert W. Aycock. The A1-Es were nicknamed the "flying dump truck or Hobo," however, over the Truong Son Mountains the attack aircraft took the call sign "Sandy." Sandy's were usually in the role of escorts for combat search and rescue helicopters. Kilbourne and Aycock were veteran pilots getting along in their Air Force careers. In short, they were very much like the aircraft they flew, time tested with many victories to their credit. They immediately gave the North Vietnamese a dose of their 20 MM cannons and rockets. Hill 891 was one chaotic nightmare for those on the ground.

For the forward air controller, Covey 57, losing focus now could lead to a huge disaster. He continued to orchestrate the Gladiator gunships and the Sandy A1-Es. He had his "shit tightly wired together." Fuel consumption and ordnance usage now had to be considered. The Spartan rescue helicopters now had to be called on to slip into the maelstrom and pick up the recon team.

The plan for the pick up was a simple one. The gunships would lead the Slicks in, shooting as they went. The Slicks would land/hover and take on the recon team and take off. A request from the gunships to turn on their lights was heeded by Woolridge and Zanow's helo, but Taylor and Williams's ship remained blackened out. The gunships were concerned that friendly fire could come into play with 4 helos working in close proximity and a night that was darker than normal. Recon team Flatfoot would mark their position with a hand held strobe light so the air assets could identify the friendlies.

With the clock ticking and fuel being consumed, Covey 57 radioed instructions for Ira Taylor and Ralph Williams' Spartan 52 to begin their run to pick up the beleaguered recon team. Kent Woolridge and William Zanow's helo was right on their heels. Ducking parachute flares and North Vietnamese machine gun fire, Ira Taylor piloted his Huey through the gauntlet the enemy had waiting. Grounding one skid runner and keeping the other off the downside slope, Taylor recounted: "I landed and 3 Nungs from the recon team wasted no time climbing aboard. They were quickly followed by 2 Special Forces soldiers." It appeared there was some confusion among the recon team as to who was getting on the first Huey out. Master Sergeant Baxter quickly pointed out the team members he wanted to board Taylor's Slick. Taylor ordered his crew chief to "get them all on board; we are on our way out!" He quickly brought the Huey's engine RPMs up for take off when his right side door gunner opened up with a burst of fire from his .50 caliber machine gun. Even before the burst was finished someone screamed "stop firing, stop firing." The voice on Taylor's head set was coming from one of the Gladiator gunships who felt friendly fire was coming far too close. Taylor yelled to the door gunner to cease fire. The gunner replied that there were enemy soldiers within 100 feet of the Spartan. Taylor sneaked a quick peek to his right and there outlined by the light of a descending flare was a North Vietnamese soldier staring directly into the cockpit. The only thing separating Ira Taylor and Ralph Williams from a burst of AK-47 fire was a brittle piece of Plexiglas. The pilot furiously worked both hands and feet and the Huey lunged forward and upward. The Spartan grabbed the unwanted attention of every bad guy on the side of Hill 891. Everything from AK-47 tracers to rocket propelled grenades went over, under, and around the escaping helo. While Taylor and Williams situation was dicey at best, the second Huey piloted by Woolridge and Zanow had already tangled with the North Vietnamese.

Huey crew of ill-fated Spartan 53. Photo taken on November 5, 1967 at Phu Bai two days prior to mission over Hill 891. L to R—Aircraft Commander Kent Woolridge, Sp. 4 Jarvis (gunner), Warrant Officer 1 co-pilot Bill Zanow, Sp. 5 Bill Whitney (crew chief). Photo courtesy of Kent Woolridge.

Gaining some altitude, Ira Taylor's Spartan 52 began to get a better focus on the area surrounding the recon team and what Taylor's door gunner saw was truly shocking. He claimed to have seen Woolridge and Zanow's ship hit by enemy ground fire and roll onto its back. Taylor himself caught a fleeting glimpse of Wooldridge's landing light pointing skyward. The light was designed to shine downward to illuminate landing zones. The North Vietnamese gunners had claimed their second helo, the first being the Vietnamese Air Force Kingbee that crashed only 3 miles from Hill 891 and whose fate was still unknown to those on or around Hill 891.

Ira Taylor coaxed his ship out of the kill zone. He had wounded aboard and his fuel situation did not permit him the opportunity to make a pass over the remaining recon team or Woolridge's crash site. He headed Spartan 52 for Hue Phu Bai Hospital knowing the prospects for the survival of any of Woolridge's crew was slim. The Huey had been shot down, rolled down the mountainside and came to rest in a pile of shattered Plexiglas, aluminum and wiring harnesses. The sickening sight was reminiscent of a scene recreated in Apocalypse Now.

The mountainside was crawling with North Vietnamese regulars who had withstood the furious air attacks of the Army Gladiators and Air Force Skyraiders whose ordnance had undoubtedly killed their fellow soldiers. Had any Americans survived the wreck they could only expect the obvious treatment. Uncle Ho's Army had a very dubious reputation when it came to prisoners of war. It seems the rules laid out in the Geneva Convention had not been required reading for the NVA.

The pilots flying over 891 all reported a disturbing message delivered by Bruce Baxter in a very matter-of-fact voice that his team continued to take heavy incoming fire. Baxter's self control and professionalism continued to amaze both pilots and crews desperately trying to relieve the pressure on Flatfoot. Another amazing thing was how tenacious the NVA was even after being pounded from the air. Often the mere sight of two Air Force Skyraiders and 2 Army attack helicopter gunships (Gladiators) would persuade the NVA to break off and continue their southbound trek. This encounter seemed more significant than what was normally experienced on or around the Ho Chi Minh Trail in Laos.

Each passing hour seemed to bring more NVA troops along with heavier guns—guns that could reach aircraft travelling at 300 miles per hour. The Americans responded by also upping the ante with added air assets. Wasn't this supposed to be a secret war? Should the proverbial cat get out of the bag, the American public would be bombarded by the anti-war crowd. Needless to say, Ho Chi Minh was not intimated by college students, "Hollyweirds" or the media. Unlike the fickle American politicians, Ho's only restraints came from the suppliers of his war materiel, the Soviet Union and China. Should Ho's policies displease them, his civil war would be disemboweled. It was, therefore, beneficial to Ho Chi Minh to keep the Laotian and Cambodian trespassing under wraps so as not to upset the world community. Keeping things on the QT was just about the only thing the U.S. and North Vietnam agreed upon; it was beneficial to both.

Monk and Farmer's mini-gun hadn't even cooled from their firing run when their radio came to life with the hushed sounds of Bruce Baxter's voice. Still fighting off the shock of witnessing the sickening sight of Zanow and Woolridge's crash, the two Gladiator pilots could not afford themselves the luxury of feeling remorse for those Farmer feared "would surely be killed in the crash." Baxter's voice was muffled and nearly a whisper but what he had to say shocked both of the Gladiator crews and served to remind them that the mission was far from completed. Bruce Baxter's whispered request was for the Army gunships to "fire directly at our own strobe light." Don Monk knew that the enemy was within yards of Flatfoot's position and he maneuvered his gunship into position for yet another firing run. Baxter's request could mean only one thing—his team was on the brink of annihilation. It was a lot to ask of the 20 year-old pilots. The Army pilots had performed brilliantly, but to fire on their own countrymen; to possibly kill them in order to save them . . . no one was trained for this mission. The Gladiator and Spartan crews had proven "they were good pilots too."

Their guns and ordnance were quickly readied when two voices interrupted. The first was that of Covey 57 and the second of a newcomer to the scene, Air Force rescue helicopter call sign Jolly Green 29.

CHAPTER 6

JOLLY 26 RETURN TO BASE

Da Nang Air Base, SVN, 23:07 hours, 8 November, 1967

The tune wafting through the "Doom Club's" screened windows was the unmistakable caterwauling of Mick Jaeger and his Rolling Stones. A watering hole frequented by U.S.A.F. pilots, the Doom Club featured much more than Jaeger's lyrics. It also hosted "talented" young dancers whose gyrations could take a thirsty pilot far away. For those not on "standby" and whose latest mission was history, a J.D. and coke or Budweiser could help pass time and wash down the dust and aviation fumes.

The club's walls had been festooned by the pilots with photos of their aircraft and beloved crews. The Doom Club was an oasis where reminiscing about past missions, close calls, and fallen friends could be discussed and shared with comforting friends. However, neither Keith Richards nor Mick Jaeger's tunes could block out the knowledge that there would be more missions yet to fly. There would be hairy and dangerous missions with absolutely no predictability. The hand of fate or luck could intercede or more preferably the hand of God. Too soon the pilots/music aficionados would have to return to their chosen professions where the thumping of rotor blades would replace Charlie Watt's percussion talent and tepid canteen water would be a far cry from a J.D. and Coke.

The Da Nang Air Base was a sprawling complex. It served as home to numerous types of aircraft and the pilots and crews of the U.S.A.F. The sleek and sexy F-4 Phantom flew out of Da Nang, as did the powerful

C-130 Hercky Bird and the V.N.A.F. Kingbee helicopters. Also home to the HH-3E "Jolly Green Giant," the rescue helicopter designed and manufactured by Sikorsky Company for the sole purpose of rescuing those in peril. The big bird had a stellar record for dependability and performance and "Jolly" crews had confidence in it and their own ability to fly the massive helo.

At 2307 hours (11:07 pm civilian time) the word was passed down to the flight line to ready two Jolly's, call signs #26 and #29. Both Jollys had Alpha One status, meaning each had been designated good to go by their flight engineers, Eugene L. Clay for 26 and Alvin Malone for J.G. 29.

The J.G.'s would remain on alert for 24 hours. Pilots and crews would have to remain available at a moments notice. The four pilots (1 pilot and 1 copilot per helo) were summoned for a briefing on the mission they had caught. Both aircraft had been started and cocked into the wind in preparation for the mission. The pilots were told that a SOG recon team had declared a Prairie Fire Emergency and they had to be extracted immediately. Jolly Green 29 would be piloted by Capt. Jack McTasney and Jolly Green 26 would be commanded by Capt. Gerald O. Young. Both were experienced and knew SOG's reputation for poking the proverbial stick into the hornet's nest. The mission would take them into a "denied" area on or near the Ho Chi Minh Trail. SOGs reputation for finding trouble and danger in Laos was already known to the professional pilots. The Doom Club would have to be put on hold.

Both crews completed their personal preparation. McTasney pulled on his flight suit followed by his survival vest. He checked the government issued .38 caliber revolver and slid it into the holster under his arm. He allowed himself one thought: "We are in deep shit now!" The shock of being ordered into life threatening situations was tempered by the many tasks it took to fly the massive helo. The preparation, demands of flying, and the desperate situation those in need of help found themselves in overwhelmed the danger about to be encountered.

There seemed to be a sharper edge to this mission. "Blue Chip" himself wanted the aircraft launched now! General William S. "Spike" Momeyer was "Blue Chip," the 7th Air Force Commander. What he meant by now could actually be interpreted as *before* now. The General, putting his weight behind a rescue mission, seemed more than odd. Occasionally missions would be scrubbed due to weather, other resources completing the rescue or a dozen other reasons. Only Momeyer himself could call off this mission and that seemed very unlikely.

Lifting off, the two rescue helos were granted permission to gain altitude. After reading their instruments, the helos took a westerly heading towards Laos and Hill 891. With the copilots reading their maps and working the radios they began to piece together the details (what there were) concerning their rescue mission.

The Doom Club was soon left in the exhaust of the Sikorsky engines and the Jollys continued west and slightly north. After several minutes the Da Nang tower came on the Jolly's radios with a rather puzzling message. "Jolly 26 this is tower. Blue Chip orders you to R.T.B. (return to base)." The message was quickly followed by Jolly 29 requesting 26 go to company frequency and then requesting 26 as back up on this one. "No sweat 29, Jolly 26 agrees. Let's go back to tower frequency." 26 then informed the Da Nang tower that "we are going with 29." The tower failed to respond to J.G. 26's assertion that they would continue on, and neither McTasney nor Young returned to the radio again regarding 26's status. It was a bizarre exchange in which a Captain's request for assistance outweighed a General's order. It was also curious that operating only one Jolly was suddenly acceptable procedure. Standard operating procedure called for two Jollies operating together. It was just one of many incidents that would raise questions when the situation on Hill 891 was concluded. Was the long reach of fate tapping the J.G. pilots on the shoulder or was it nothing at all? One thing was for sure, the two Jollys pressed on towards Master Sergeant Bruce Baxter's beleaguered recon team.

The SOG team in peril was west of the Ashau Valley and had been operating in the Truong Son Mountains. They were clearly inside Laotian borders. The Ashau Valley rested on the eastern edge of the Ho Chi Minh Trail (see map) and the area had been used for nearly 8 years by North Vietnam to smuggle weapons and ammunition into the south. The area was known to J.G. (Jolly Green) crews as being active with NVA and the mountains in the area reached to 3,000 foot altitudes. Both of these conditions were worth noting. In addition, night was upon them and fuel demands had to be considered while operating in mountainous areas. The pilots were aware of the conditions and the effects they had on their aircraft. Experience was on the Jollys side. What was unknown to the J.G. pilots was the steep slope the recon team was pinned to, and the building concentration of NVA and heavy guns that changed by the hour. As information trickled in on JG 29's radio, Jack McTasney's instincts assessed the situation correctly and prompted his comment that "things just got worse with this mission."

Jerry Clearman was Jolly 29's copilot. Working the radio he successfully connected with Covey 57, the forward air controller already on the scene. His counterpart on Jolly 26 was Ralph Brower. Both Clearman and Brower had previously flown C-141s and then switched over to Jolly Greens. Clearman and McTasney had crossed paths at Sheppard AFB in Texas. McTasney had served as Clearman's instructor pilot when Clearman was converting from C-141s to Jolly Greens. The two copilots brought lots of experience into the Jolly's cockpits. This experience allowed both pilots to concentrate on flying the helos with the confidence that other tasks were in good hands.

Jolly Green 29s crew of McTasney, Clearman, Sergeant Alvin A. Malone (flight engineer) and John H. Stemple (Pararescue) was first rate. Leadership from the cockpit, technical training, and motivation were all characteristics shared by the crew. In just a short amount of time, 29's crew would need every bit of talent and resources they had collectively accumulated.

Closing in on Hill 891, the rescue helos were advised by Covey 57 that Blind Bat was dropping parachute flares. The position of the gladiators (Army attack helos) was also noted, as was the absence of A1-E Skyraiders, the prop driven aircraft of Korean War vintage that were often paired with the rescue helos and were not yet back on station and presumably refueling. Jolly 29 rogered (he received) Covey's message and asked Covey why there was mumbling on this frequency. With the busy skies over the recon team, clarity, brevity, and self-restraint was a must. It all came down to self-discipline and radio restraint. Covey addressed the mumbling, "That's Flatfoot (recon team). They are whispering because the hostiles are in close and using rifle grenades." Covey also advised the Jollys to "stay high until I clear you in." Each aircraft pilot and crewman had to rely on the skill of Covey and he had to depend on each pilot's airmanship and discipline to pull off a successful conclusion. Any miscommunication or act of self-indulgence by any of the aircraft commanders could make this a disaster of far greater magnitude than it already was. The pressure to perform was immense. At this time, Covey 57 shouldered the burden. With his confidence and professionalism he manipulated his available resources for the best possible outcome. (Covey 57's name has not been discovered.)

The calming and reassuring voice of Covey 57 broke radio silence, "Jolly 29 this is Covey. We have already had two helos shot down, do you read?" "Roger Covey 57, Jolly 29 copies. Two helos down." The conversation continued when McTasney asked, "Are there survivors or wounded?" Covey 57 replied: "Five, both Americans are wounded."

Based on the information Covey provided and their on the scene assessment, the J.G. pilots began to form a plan to rescue the remnants of recon team Flatfoot. Jollys were outfitted with a powerful winch operated by the flight engineer; however, using the winch was never an option and was quickly ruled out. Hovering over the five survivors would take too long and make the Jolly and its crew a sitting duck for the NVA gunners. Watching the steady stream of green tracers that hounded the Army Gladiators on each of their firing runs and with the knowledge that two helos were already down was proof enough this rescue had to be done quickly and with as much movement as possible. The NVA below had earned their marksmanship badges and were mad as hell at being pounded from above. It was quite apparent that both sides had locked horns, and that neither was going to leave the battlefield. The NVA, like a shark, sensed blood in the water and had already experienced some success. American participants would not leave their recon team to be overrun. Something had to give. For the NVA to spend this much time and lives in pursuit of a recon team was not a normal response. They also began pursuing long after darkness had set in. This was a violation of their established routine. Clearly this was a well trained and armed NVA. The U.S., too, was sending assets far beyond what would be considered normal, although nothing was ever "normal" operating in Laos. After all, this was Colby's Secret War, continually committing aircraft and losing lives would not help in keeping the "secret." Would a point be reached when the rescue effort was denied resources and the helos were recalled?

Fuel now became an issue for the J.G.s along with the changing light conditions and the steep slope. Flatfoot would have to be rescued by landing on the ground. McTasney had to make the extraction immediately, requesting Blind Bat (flare ship) to drop four flares on McTasney's command and then refrain from any more drops. Jack McTasney was hoping to mess up the NVA's vision by going from dark to light, sometimes referred to as night vision or "night lights." As the flares burned, Jolly 29 would swoop in while the NVA was adjusting to the light conditions. The survivors would be scooped up and everyone could RTB (return to base). Blind Bat rogered 29 and agreed to "wait for your call."

In a recent rescue attempt a Jolly pilot had been shot through the neck. That incident prompted Jack McTasney to dispatch flight engineer Alvin Malone to break out chest plates (armor) for the exposed pilots. P.J. John Stemple brought two M-16s (rifles) with fully loaded magazines into the cockpit as ordered. Stemple was on the diminutive side, but a feisty guy who was never bashful when it came to using the M-60 machine gun. He was also the NCOIC (non commissioned officer in charge) of P.J.s at Da Nang. Pararescue was still a bastion for N.C.Os and few officers had infiltrated its ranks. One final precaution was taken—both the interior and exterior lights on Jolly 29 were shut off with the approval of the entire crew. There was no need to advertise the Jolly's whereabouts.

J.G. 26 (Gerald Young) interrupted 29's radio silence. "Understand you are going into the L.Z., we are ready too." J.G. 29 responded by advising J.G. 26 to "stay high." The Army gunships (Gladiators) were monitoring the conversation between the rescue helos (26 & 29) and advised: "Jolly 29 we have you in sight, follow us in." However, there was a conspicuous absence of the U.S.A.F.'s versatile A1-E Skyraiders. It prompted Captain McTasney to comment, "A1-Es were not there when I was and I am not sure why not." There was no time to wait for more attack aircraft to arrive. The Huey gunships "were low on ammo" and McTasney opted to attempt the rescue "now." McTasney was impressed with the way the Army pilots had assessed the situation and commented, "damn you guys are good!" Flying in to pick up Flatfoot while the Gladiators hosed down the NVA on the mountainside was a huge advantage that did not go unnoticed by the J.G. crews. Calling Blind Bat for the flare drop, the entire contingent of Army gunships (2) and J.G. 29 plunged into the soupy mixture of smoke, shadows and darkness. The only thing missing was Wagner's "Flight of the Valkyrie."

Only one hundred feet above the mountainside McTasney and Clearman spotted the sickening sight of Kent Woolridge and Bill Zanow's Huey lying unceremoniously in a pile of twisted aluminum and shattered plexi-glass. The pile belched smoke but fire and flames were absent. No sooner had the wrecked Huey been sighted when the sound of small arms fire was heard and the voice of Flight Engineer Alvin Malone came on the head set. "Pilot we are taking ground fire," "pilot copies ground fire" was acknowledgement from the cockpit. The rotor blades began to stir up a blizzard of loose vegetation and dust as the rescue helo neared the L.Z. In addition to the storm stirred up by the rotors, the flares began to float ever so slowly into the L.Z. area creating moving shadows and adding to the confusion. Jolly 29's front and left landing gears depressed as they touched down on the upside of the mountain. McTasney's Jolly had landed in Dante's Inferno. No sooner had the gears touched down when five guys in what resembled black pajamas and boonie hats appeared. Crouched low, their packs were clearly visible they moved towards the Jolly. Two appeared to be wounded. McTasney continued the struggle to keep the helo level and the rotors from striking the ground. The RT worked their way to the left side of the aircraft. The pilot quickly dispatched P.J. John Stemple telling him to get out and move them (the RT) to the cargo door on the right side of the helo. Stemple did not respond, but it appeared to McTasney that bodies were being pulled on board. The communication lines from the cockpit to the flight engineer (Malone) and the P.J. (Stemple) had been shot out and any "word" would have to be passed directly from man to man.

The Air Force rescue helicopter had only one door on the right side. RTs were not accustomed to working with the JG's configuration and that accounted for the delay in getting the recon team on the rescue helo.

Small arms fire broke out again. The NVA riflemen were well within AK-47 range and began to hammer the Sikorsky made helo. The latest volley triggered a yellow flashing light in the cockpit's main caution panel. The J.G. began to behave erratically and the pilots struggled to keep the Jolly in a hover. Jerry Clearman (copilot) prepared to use manual controls in the event the electronics failed.

Sitting in the right seat and situated up slope, Jerry Clearman presented a fine target for any NVA rifleman that was foolish enough to expose himself and take careful aim. The copilot remained focused despite the increased volume of fire the Jolly was absorbing. The erratic behavior of the aircraft now demanded the entire attention of both pilots. J.G. 29 shuddered and rocked as one of the Army Gladiators cruised directly overhead, clearing the Jolly by only twenty five feet. As if the speed of the Gladiator and its rotor wash weren't enough, the attack helo was laying down a heavy dose of belt fed grenades and the impact from the explosions could be felt inside the Jolly. The noise inside the Jolly came to a crescendo when P.J. John Stemple opened up with his .50 caliber machine gun in an effort to keep the NVA from closing on the Jolly.

McTasney needed no more convincing. It was time to get the hell out of there. He depressed the right foot peddle and the Jolly began to move downhill, gaining altitude if only slightly. Before traveling two hundred feet the red fire light flashed and the cockpit filled with fuel vapors, but neither pilot elected to shut down an engine at this point. As if there weren't enough chaos inside the helo, Flight Engineer, Alvin Malone, informed the pilots "We've only got three survivors on board and we are leaking fuel into the cargo compartment. Don't let anyone light up"—as if anyone smoked during sex or while being shot at. Just as the helo's intercom failed the radio came alive. "Covey this is Flatfoot one zero." It was Master Sergeant Bruce Baxter. "My radioman and I are still on the ground." Baxter and Kussick had not made it aboard J.G. 29. Both pilots were stunned. The Jolly had taken a horrific pounding; fuel was leaking and a power shortage left the veteran pilots with only one call. McTasney announced: "I can't go back into the L.Z." A short pause followed before the radio once again came alive. This time it was Gerald Young's voice "Jolly 29 this is 26, we are going in after the remainder of Flatfoot." "Roger 26, this is 29 climbing out, be advised we took heavy ground fire—advise you not go in."

Jolly 29's entire crew received some positive news when Flight Engineer, Alvin Malone, announced he had successfully stemmed the flow of fuel emptying into the cargo bay. Staff Sergeant Malone may have saved the day with his McGyver-like thinking and his willingness to sacrifice a perfectly good t-shirt. The Jolly did not need to lose fuel and most certainly did not want it inside the helo. The good news was short lived. Instrument lights winked on and off indicating one engine was receiving twice the fuel flow needed and its tank empty while the other engine's fuel flow was zero. Only 600 lbs of fuel remained. Jerry Clearman checked his map and fixed a heading for the nearest "friendly" base, hoping the badly mauled Jolly 29 could be nursed long enough to make it. The best hope for 29 was Khe Sanh Marine Base. Clearman had the fate of the entire crew in his hands. A miscalculation under these circumstances and yet another helo would be lost. As it turned out Captain Clearman was right on the money with his selection of Khe Sanh. It was the very place General William Westmoreland had chosen to fight the "mother of all battles," the very place America could sucker the NVA forces to mass and then use our superior technology to crush them in one set piece battle. In the meantime the Marines would be dangled like bait to keep the NVA attention and screw up their logistical situation in their movement south.

Khe Sanh was a living hell for the stubborn "Devil Dogs" who lived a rat-like existence-eating, fighting, and sleeping beneath the surface of the red clay. Clearman estimated it would take a twenty minute flight to the beleaguered base. While battling hydraulic, electronic, and mechanical problems, Jack McTasney eavesdropped on a conversation between Covey 57 and the ever present Gladiator gun ships. J.G. 26 had made it into the L.Z. and Young and Brower had their cargo door up slope. Covey added that 26 had the survivors aboard. Given the circumstances, it was the best that could be expected. J.G. 26 still had to get out of the L.Z.

Once again Covey 57 returned to the radio. "Jolly 26 your left engine is on fire!" The next transmission from Covey was devastating. "Jolly 26 just rolled over and slid down slope." McTasney copied the transmission from Covey; however, it was clear copilot Jerry Clearman was on a different frequency and was not privy to the devastatingly sad news. Clearman's best friend, copilot Ralph Brower, was onboard J.G. 26. McTasney could not share the bad news with his crew as J.G. 29 was locked in a life and death struggle of their own. Even if J.G. 29 had the power to reach Khe Sanh they still had to find it and land. The airstrip at Khe Sanh was used to resupply the base with the necessities—ammo, rations, and medical supplies. Reinforcements trickled in and there never seemed to be a shortage of casualties to evacuate. The other potential problem that might make 29s landing difficult was if the base was currently under attack. The airstrip always received its share of "incoming" (NVA shells). Khe Sanh was a muddy stink hole during the rainy season and a red dust bowl during the dry season. It was situated at an elevation just below mountain top level and at no time did it ever possess any aesthetic value. It was destined to become part of the "Corps" impressive history of courage and tenacity. World War I Marines had Belleau Wood, World War II Marines had Iwo Jima, and Korean Marines had the Chosen Reservoir. Vietnam era Marines would lay claim to Khe Sanh.

The Marines operating out of Khe Sanh ran patrols, set ambushes, and created logistical problems for the NVA in the area. The NVA grew tired of the Marine presence and laid siege to Khe Sanh mortaring Marine positions and probing Marine perimeters. Pressure from the NVA only stiffened the "jar heads" resolve to remain in what some thought was an untenable position. Neither the Corp's storied history nor their stubbornness would permit them to leave, and certainly General William Westmoreland was the driving force keeping the Marines at a rather weak position. Westmoreland felt that ". . . clandestine teams operating cross border in Laos . . ." needed Khe Sanh held and he also felt that ". . . to relinquish this area would be a major propaganda victory for the enemy." President Johnson was concerned that Khe Sanh would "turn into our Dien Bien Phu." Everyone seemed to be fixated on Khe Sanh. This is where J.G. 29 was headed; it was their only choice albeit a dangerous one.

Clearman tried to radio Khe Sanh prior to their arrival but was unable to get the tower (a general moniker for air control) at the Marine base. The Marines were hunkered down for the night and weren't expecting any air traffic. Records from King Log Events (Rescue Control Center-Saigon) indicate that at 0050 hours a request was made to "alert Khe Sanh to provide cover for JG 29 and to turn on the field lights." Whether this request was made cannot be confirmed. Finally a voice responded to Clearman. "This is Khe Sanh tower, our runway lights are inop (not working). We are on emergency power, over." Clearman answered. "Khe Sanh this is Jolly Green 29 declaring an emergency. We have to land, over." "Jolly 29 do you see a light? It's a work stand on the ramp, over." "Tower, Jolly 29, we have a light in sight."

The tower began flashing a "very" light (strobe light), and the Jolly acknowledged having a visual on the flashing beacon. With fuel critically low, McTasney cork screwed 29 towards terra firma and feeling slightly relieved with two lights to use as references, he began his landing procedures. The panel directly in front of the pilot now began flashing orange and red lights (like Xmas at a double wide) warning of immediate disaster. With only two hundred feet left McTasney called for the landing and flood lights to be turned on. Trenches and fighting holes could be seen from inside the Jolly. A few Marine grunts scurried out of the way so as not to be squashed by the J.G. Pulling the collective, and "milking" the descent without pulling down the rotor and engine RPMs, the J.G. touched down and skidded along, crushing empty ammo boxes and dozing into concertina wire before coming to a halt at the very edge of the PSP (perforated steel plates) ramp. Ever the professional, McTasney ordered the crew to begin the routine shutdown check list. The pilot himself was required to brake the rotor. As he had done hundreds of times before, Jack McTasney pulled on the brake handle but the rotors continued to spin. A closer look revealed the hydraulic line above the pilot's head had been severed by a bullet. Both the crew and RT survivors evacuated the aircraft because of the danger of fire.

For McTasney and Clearman's crew, the mission was over. Lives had been saved, heroes born, medals would be bestowed. (However, the unknown fate of J.G. 26 weighed heavily on the hearts of each crew member.) After inspection, the J.G. 29 was found to have thirty holes of various diameters sprinkled liberally from forward to aft. The Air Force sent out a team of aviation mechanics and it was determined that the helo would have to be lifted and "slung" down to Da Nang by an H-54. One report claimed that parts were cannibalized for another helo. Captain McTasney never saw J.G. 29 after it arrived at Da Nang.

Igor Sikorsky had designed a great aircraft and the Air Force educated and trained a crew to match. Both crew and at least parts of the helo would return to what they did so professionally and courageously, saving lives. The Doom Club could now be seriously considered by the pilots of J.G. 29 when they got back to Da Nang.

Staff Sergeant Alvin Malone and Staff Sergeant John Stemple received Silver Stars for their heroics on the mission. Copilot Jerry Clearman also received a Silver Star for his participation. Captain Jack McTasney was awarded the Air Force Cross and a year later (May of 1968) he attempted to rescue the sole survivor of yet another SOG team, crash landed at Tabat firebase in the Ashau Valley and was consequently picked up by another J.G. that also crashed. For this mission he received the Silver Star. During the TET offensive McTasney flew many medivacs and participated in twelve combat saves. Late June of 1968 ended Captain McTasney's tour and he rotated home by 1971 where he became a U.S.A.F. Academy faculty member.

CHAPTER 7

FLYING ON FUMES

Hill 891 Laos, 2340 hours, 8 November, 1967

Captain Gerald O. Young had already flown a rescue mission into Laos only days before being ordered to Hill 891 to rescue recon team Flatfoot. The veteran pilot knew all the nuances of the Sikorsky built helicopter he commanded and was considered a master aviator by his fellow pilots. Sent to rescue Captain Dick Mulders and crew downed in a high mountainous jungle setting, the rescue was considered a combination of classic textbook and creative flying. Young had ordered his flight engineer to dump fuel in an effort to lighten his load. His crew then hoisted Mulder's men aboard for a hair—raising flight back to Da Nang.

Da Nang had tracked Young's mission and word had spread to pilots and crews not flying that day that Young's Jolly Green might be short on fuel on its return to base. When the Da Nang tower reported the rescue Jolly's approach a crowd gathered at the asphalt landing strip to either celebrate an incredibly triumphant and heroic rescue or witness a horrible disaster. Gerald Young did not disappoint. His fuel-starved Jolly kissed the runway without even depressing the landing gear struts. "I marveled . . . , he was flying on fumes at the end." This was high praise indeed from fellow pilot and friend Captain Jack McTasney.

On the Mission to Hill 891 Young's Jolly Green crew spanned from experienced combat veterans to green newbie. Co-pilot Ralph Brower was a former C-141 pilot who had switched over to Jolly Greens. He was an outstanding pilot in his own right. The flight mechanic was

Staff Sergeant Eugene L. Clay out of Arlington, Texas. The twenty-eight year old was the crew chief, hoist operator, and M-60 machine gunner. Flight mechanics were not along just for the ride. Their technical training was an absolute necessity. Staff Sergeant Clay could have remained a ground mechanic. It required less training and was a far safer vocation. Clay chose to fly and he understood that rescue work was inherently dangerous.

The youngest member of Young's crew was Sergeant Larry W. Maysey. The Pararescue specialist had graduated from West Morris Regional High School in Chester, New Jersey, only two years prior to being sent to Viet Nam. He had survived eighteen months of the Air Force's "pipeline" training and had won the right to wear the maroon beret. With "Elvis" good looks, a hot looking hippie girlfriend and a sports car, he was as cool as it got. There was no recruiting poster for the Air Force's P.J. (para jumper) program but had there been Maysey would have been a perfect fit. Maysey had been in country for only a month.

Co-pilot Ralph Brower had listened to the many radio transmissions that had been exchanged over Hill 891. He had heard Baxter's and Kussick's reports, Covey 57s management skills, and the Gladiator and Spartan pilots sharing information. Brower and Young already knew how difficult it was going to be to rescue Kussick and Baxter. It must be kept in mind that Jolly Greens were regularly subjected to dangerous and challenging situations. Search and rescue missions seldom had weather, terrain or distance working for them. Those in need of rescue were often far out at sea, stranded on a mountain top, or hopelessly lost in a jungle. In Flatfoot's case the scenario was even more dangerous with the formidable resistance being applied by the North Vietnamese troops who had made it crystal clear they were going to oppose each rescue attempt. The final decision to attempt a rescue and place the Jolly's crew and the helo itself in jeopardy rested squarely on the shoulders of Captains Young and Brower. The entire four man crew had volunteered for SAR (search and rescue) work and their pilots were experienced and skilled aviators. Both Young and Brower were highly educated and mature professionals. It was not their first rodeo.

By listening to the radio calls, Brower had established that both Kussick and Baxter were wounded but alive. It was also clear that their situation was becoming more desperate by the minute. Baxter's request to have the Gladiators fire on his own position was proof that time was running out. As Monk's gunship passed below, the Jolly Green co-pilot Cletus Farmer had just "tightened his circle of fire" around the two Green Beret's position, ". . . so close that after releasing the trigger I was unable to breathe until I heard Flatfoot on the radio again." Gerald Young could not leave the two Special Forces men to be killed by the NVA. He had watched McTasney work his J.G. in and out of trouble. He and Brower would have to do the same. Jolly Green 26 represented the last best chance for Joseph Kussick and Bruce Baxter to leave Hill 891 alive.

Two Vietnamese Air Force helos, two American Hueys and one Jolly Green had already attempted to extract or had succeeded in extracting parts of recon team Flatfoot. Gerald O Young had decided to close the deal. He would follow one of the Gladiators into the landing zone site. Eugene Clay manned the M-60 machine gun on the right side and Larry Maysey did the same on the left providing some formidable fire power for J.G. 26. The hoist was a non-factor. The NVA fire power had completely ruled out the helo going into a hover. The mountainside flashed by as J.G. 26 approached the landing zone.

Captain Jack McTasney offered this scenario based on his extensive experience and the radio traffic he monitored. "I think Young and Brower hit a hover over the landing zone, made a 180º turn putting the cargo door upslope (Maysey's side) and resting the right main landing gear on the ground." McTasney reported hearing Captain Young say "both Kussick and Baxter were on board." This was corroborated by other pilots on the scene. It is not completely clear how Baxter and Kussick got into Jolly 26. Air Force records indicate that P.J. Larry Maysey was dispatched and somehow aided the two wounded SOG men into the passenger compartment. In either case the PJ's job would be to render medical attention to the wounded. This would have been top priority for Maysey. The Air Force officially concluded that P.J. Maysey exited the aircraft and assisted both wounded Special Forces men. For his action under fire, Maysey would receive the Air Force Cross, thereby joining only a handful of enlisted men to do so.

Young's Jolly now faced the same withering torrent of lead that McTasney's had only minutes earlier. Jolly 26 initiated its takeoff. Unlike Jolly 29, which took off with its nose down slope, Young and Brower chose to take off parallel to the mountainside. McTasney noted that the greatest volume of fire originated from downhill so flying into the fire may have provided a more difficult target. It is possible Young's takeoff provided a greater mass to shoot at, but this is only speculation.

The Jolly presented a large target and was slow on takeoff. ADF (altitude density factor) also prevented the helo from ascending as rapidly as Young would have wanted. A murderous volley followed J.G. 26 out of the landing zone, some from point blank range. Despite the pounding, the Gladiators and Skyraiders had administered the NVA were relentless and refused to release their steely grip on Jolly 26.

Young and Brower sensed the intensity and wrath of the NVA assault and wasted no time beginning their departure. Only seconds after lifting off their right engine belched a wisp of smoke and then burst into flames. No fewer than three pilots reported the engine fire and also witnessed the Jolly become inverted, fall on its back and slam down hard on the steep slope. The fire then spread from the engine and engulfed the entire aircraft. An explosion of sorts accompanied the fire.

Warrant Officer Kent Woolridge, who's Huey had also been shot down, now became an eye witness to the entire odyssey of Jolly 26. The following is Warrant Officer Kent Woolridge's report: "He came to a hover, made a slight left turn and his gear struts compressed as he landed. Immediately tracers (NVA) started bouncing off his rotor system. He came off the ground, dropped the nose and rose about sixty feet into his departure path. Suddenly the nose of the aircraft pitched up and J.G. 26 slid aft. It descended tail first until the aircraft contacted the ground and exploded in flames."

The number of Americans unaccounted for continued to increase. How many survivors, how many casualties and how many dead were completely unknown. In addition, the steep side of Hill 891 was quickly becoming a junkyard for Army and Air Force Helos.

<u>What was known</u>
Hill 891, Laos, 2329 hours, 8 November, 1967

By 11:30 pm civilian time it had been established that the crew of Jolly Green 26 which included Captain Young, Copilot Ralph Brower, Flight Engineer Eugene Clay and P.J. Larry Maysey had successfully reached Master Sergeant Bruce Baxter and Specialist 4 Joseph Kussick.

They had lifted off and reportedly been shot down; the status of all aboard was unknown. It was possible some of the rescuers would now need rescuing. The NVA could also lay claim to the UH-1D Huey that crashed without burning. Pilots Kent Woolridge and Bill Zanow, along with Crew Chief Bill Whitney and door gunner Specialist 4 Jarvis, were all on the side of the mountain. Their status was also unclear. In addition, the Vietnamese Air Force Kingbee had crash landed several miles away.

If not for the superior efforts of Jack McTasney and Jerry Clearman, J.G. 29 would also have been lost. As it was, the Jolly was unflyable and had barely made it back to Marine base Khe Sanh where it was found to have nearly thirty holes in it. Despite the monumental efforts of the Army and Air Force, ten Americans were totally unaccounted for. Two helo crews and remnants of recon team Flatfoot had reportedly crashed. Damage to aircraft both on and off the scene was significant, as was the fuel consumed and ordnance expended. There was no end in sight. Rescuing a recon team was one thing; rescuing or recovering the rescuers was quite another.

What would it take to bring the debacle on Hill 891 to a conclusion, and who would make the decision to risk more American lives to complete the mission? In the morning hours of 9 November 1967, someone in Da Nang authorized three more Jolly Greens to be scrambled and sent to Hill 891, or so they thought. Apparently the decision to risk more Americans and helicopters had been made by General Spike Momeyer (Blue Chip) who must have been anxious to learn the fate of Captain Young's crew and aircraft.

The three Jollys set a course for the "denied" territory inside neutral Laos with Hill 891 as their destination. Approximately ten minutes into the trip two Jollys were advised to break off and proceed "up north." This left Jolly Green 04 piloted by Captain Vern Dander to proceed on to Hill 891 unaccompanied. The Air Force usually worked their helos in pairs in what the pilots referred to as "high and low bird." Dander flew his helo solo for the remainder of the trip to Hill 891 somewhat puzzled as to why the "high and low bird" doctrine had suddenly been "shit canned." Upon arriving over Hill 891 Captain Dander realized he had either found the crash site of Jolly 26 or he had flown into "hell on earth." He was relieved to see the A1-E Skyraiders already on the scene although they seemed to hardly notice him while they were delivering their assortment of terrifying ordnances to the mountainside and hopefully on top of the NVA who prowled the face of the mountain.

It is worthy to note that on the evening of November 9, 1967, an Air Force F-4 Phantom had been shot down north of Hill 891 at Ban Lowboy Ford, also in Laos. The fighter/bomber was on a bombing run and inexplicably crashed into a mountainside. Both the Soviets and Chinese (fighting a war by proxy) had continually supplied the NVA with more sophisticated anti-aircraft equipment that had caught up to the American attack aircraft's once superior technology. However, on this occasion, fellow Air Force pilots in both an F-4 and a FAC (02) could not account for what actually took out the F-4; nor did they see any parachutes deploy. Nevertheless the Search and Rescue (SAR) automatically kicked into gear. It wasn't until hours later that the voice of Lieutenant Lance Sijan was heard and authenticated. Malcolm McConnell's book, Into the Mouth of The Cat, chronicles Sijan's epic struggle for which he would be awarded the Congressional Medal of Honor.

The rescues on Hill 891 and at Ban Loboy Ford were probably seen by the rescuers as having very little in common. However, they shared some of the same days and hours, and it cannot be disputed that both required the identical assets: Jolly Green helos, A1-E attack aircraft, C-130s and F-4 phantoms. More importantly both required the utmost care and vigilance by the rescuers, as the NVA always took advantage of these situations. U.S. history is replete with stories of the efforts of selflessness on the part of our rescuers to recover their comrades from enemy clutches.

Sometime following the Sijan shoot down it was discovered that the fuses on the bombs our own aircraft were carrying detonated too early causing Sijan's aircraft to crash in yet another peculiar type of "friendly fire."

Dander made his presence known to the FAC flyer and advised he was passing over the crash site. Bringing the Sikorsky built helo to top speed, Dander passed over what he felt was the crashed Jolly Green. The crew reported that they took no ground fire, and he brought the helo around for a second pass. On the second pass the Jolly flew slower and slightly lower. There were fires burning here and there presumably where the A1-Es had dropped napalm. On what Dander thought to be the crash site there was no smoke, but a large blackened area where the elephant grass had been burned off. From the perimeter of the burned out grass a Caucasian appeared and waved what appeared to be a white t-shirt then retreated to cover. One more rehearsal run turned up one additional sighting. Three white sheets of standard sized writing paper were neatly placed on top of the burned out elephant grass. Any grouping of three items was a standardized signal of distress. Now was the time for a rescue attempt and Dander advised FAC that his next run would be to retrieve the American on the ground.

Just as Dander brought J.G. 04 into position for a "pick up" (rescue) the search and rescue coordination center at Tan Son Nhut Air Base (call sign Queen) advised through their rescue central aircraft (call sign Crown 6) that J.G. 04 "should not be there in the first place" and "to get 04 out of there." Dander would not give in and requested "to go in for P/U." Crown said, "Stand by," J.G. 04 then replied, "stand by hell, let's go in for pick up." The conversation between aircraft and the numerous control centers continued for some time. Once again Captain Dander requested permission to "go in for a P/U." This time Queen advised "NEGATIVE," and again Queen was advised by yet another U.S.A.F. call sign "Hillsboro" that 04's request was "negative, negative, negative."

With all the air assets in place including F-4 fighter bombers, Covey, 4-6 A1-Es and helicopter gun ships the time was right for a rescue. Yet Dander's pleas to land were refused. To this day he cannot justify or understand why a rescue could not be made. The frustration level had to be sky high as J.G. 04 returned to base. The only thing J.G. 04 was able to return to base with was Pararescue man Angus MacDougal's 35 MM photos taken on one of the helo's several passes. It was not what the crew and pilot had hoped for.

It had taken quite a while for the pilots and Jolly crews to gain recognition for their work as search and rescue specialists. However, as more and more pilots were shot out of the sky, by more and more sophisticated NVA anti-aircraft technology, the Jolly Green crews became more widely appreciated as the highly trained professionals they were. Besides, a little loss of pride at being rescued was a far better fate than hanging from a roof rafter with your shoulders dislocated at the Hanoi Hilton.

U.S.A.F., U.S. Army, U.S.M.C Air assets and support for SAR on Hill 891

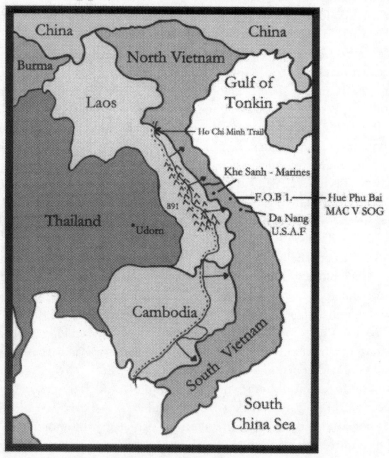

Sketch by Star Barkman.

That Empty Feeling

Captain Dander's story was bewildering at best. If Dander was accurate in his analysis of the situation, there were some very strange decisions made regarding Jolly Green 04 and its usage or lack thereof. Maybe Dander and his crew were somewhat overzealous and anxious to "make a save" and thereby disregarded their own safety. It could also be the big picture was being overlooked. The issue of secrecy and the well being of the crew were being looked after by those higher in command.

The answer may be found in a secret document now declassified known as the Mission Narrative 1-3-182. Many documents regarding the secret war in Laos and Cambodia were destroyed in 1975. However, this Mission Narrative survived and was authored by two Air Force Captains, Purvis and May.

The Mission Narrative is cluttered with an incredible amount of Air Force jargon, "Zulu times," Sandy reports, requests and a variety of radio frequencies. There are conflicting reports, unfounded reports, and corroborating reports all on a two and half page report. On the first page alone 17 different times are mentioned, 58 aircraft (many the same) and 40 call signs were cited by Captain Purvis. If the narrative were written to clarify the confusion and chaos on and over Hill 891, it failed miserably. However, this was probably not its intended purpose.

What did the narrative accomplish and untangle regarding the event on Hill 891?

- That there were 6-8 A-1E (Sandies) actively working (bombing, strafing the battle area). They also provided reports of seeing Americans on the ground. Many of the reports were repetitive due to the fact the Sandy's completed many flyovers and there were numerous Sandy's present.
- The Crown aircraft (C-130) which was a rescue control aircraft did not have FM radio capability making for communications with "Army and Marine forces, both air and ground, difficult at best."
- That two Recon teams had been inserted in the area, Bruce Baxter's Flatfoot and one other call sign, Wonderful Time. Wonderful Time's existence was confirmed by Lieutenant Dick who intercepted one of their few radio calls. "Wonderful Time" was several thousand meters from Hill 891 and managed to evade

the wrath of the NVA. That team resisted using their radio and by so doing drew no attention to themselves.
- That the Covey aircraft and the A-1Es reported no ground fire was noted.
- That the VNAF H34 helos performed extraordinarily well despite the poor communication system and their inability to receive from the Crown C-130. It raised the question; could more Americans have been saved early on?
- Finally that the failure to utilize Jolly Green 04 commanded by Captain Vern Dander was a huge mistake. Every indication was they could have affected a safe pick up. Threatening a Court Martial via radio and failing to give the on the scene Commander the power to utilize an important asset was clearly micro management.

Captain May, "the still unexplained failure to allow Jolly Green 04 to rescue an injured American resulted in his death. In addition, the failure over a period of more than four hours to follow the unanimous recommendation of the on scene commander and all forces in the SAR area to allow Jolly Green 04 to pick up the survivors was at best demoralizing to the rescue forces. The many other USAF and VNAF crews who played some part in this effort undoubtedly had their faith in our rescue capabilities severely shaken."

There is some question as to the assertion that 04's failure to pick up caused an American's death. Although no one could say for sure, some of Bulldog's men felt the American was already deceased. Again, the fog of war prevailed.

CHAPTER 8

NOT A DAY GOES BY

FOB#1 SVN

Had Hill 891 been located inside of South Vietnam, a more definitive solution could have been found. The Debacle on Hill 891 in Laos spun wildly out of control. With every passing hour more lives were lost and the status of others became unknown. The tempo of the violence continued to escalate and was evident in the number of aircraft claimed by NVA fire and the aircraft that had been damaged and were forced to leave the scene.

 The secret war in Laos had to be kept a "secret." Expanding the rescue effort might bring unwanted attention and alert the American media. The American public, college campuses, Hollyweirds, and the anti-war left might go into a feeding frenzy the likes of which had not been seen since the Civil War riots in New York City in 1862. Uncle Ho must have smelled victory in the making watching certain segments of the U.S. public intimidate the already feckless American politicians who placed arbitrary rules of engagement on American troops in South East Asia in order to appease those with anti-war sentiments.

 Along the Ho Chi Minh Trail alone Americans were dying because the full weight of our military could not be used. Ho read America like a cheap novel. And while he sent thousands of troops south, we fretted about keeping "the secret." Ho's college students were not chanting, "Hell no we won't go," and they were not carrying anti-war placards. They were too busy humping AK-47s and rocket-propelled grenade launchers through Laos and Cambodia. Hill 891 became emblematic of the entire

Vietnam War. That aside, a solution to the engagement on 891 had to be found quickly.

Forward Operating Base #1—Phu Bai, South Vietnam 0330 hours, 9 November, 1967

The sergeant of the guard moved through the darkened camp with little effort, sidestepping stacks of empty pallets, C-ration boxes, and discarded 55 gallon drums. Then Lieutenant Bill Vowell recalls FOB #1 at Phu Bai. "The quarters were made of stucco-like material initially constructed for the French troops that garrisoned the area." The French considered Vietnam a colony and exploited it for resources such as rubber and coffee. The French culture crept into the lives of the native Vietnamese, affecting religion and language, and rubbing some of the populace the wrong way. By the 1950's, French hegemony was under attack by Ho Chi Minh's forces and the French finally met their end at Dien Bien Phu.

Vowell also recalled an evening when an American guard dog wandered a little too far from the quarters and was killed by a mine left over by the French. At times the atmosphere inside the camp turned into a scene from Arizona's Tombstone. The camp at Phu Bai featured only one club for a parched Special Forces man to relax and drink the nectar of the Gods (alcohol). Here one club served all, officers, N.C.O.s and enlisted. Alcohol became the great equalizer.

When the strange bedfellows failed to observe moderation, nights seldom ended like an episode from Cheers. If someone thought he could mix the boisterous nature of N.C.O.s with the natural arrogance of officers and top it off with the inexperience of enlisted men, he really had no understanding of the ranks. The mixture became volatile when a healthy dose of the demon rum was consumed in copious quantities.

There probably weren't any studies or surveys taken concerning the rate of alcoholics that existed in the Special Forces but even they felt there might be a magnetic force that paired the two components together. The results were predictable. Loud and profane arguments erupted often settled by bare knuckled persuasion. On more than one occasion firearms were brandished, at which time the sight of a 1911 Colt .45 brought the unruly lads to their senses.

F.O.B. 1 at Phu Bai was originally built for French troops and utilized poured concrete. Sand bags were added by U.S. Special Forces. Photo courtesy of Gamble Dick.

Block building F.O.B. 1 at Phu Bai was kept void
of vegetation for security purposes.
Photo courtesy of Gamble Dick.

That being the state of affairs at F.O.B. #1, a mission seemed to be the elixir to all hard feelings and the antagonists crossed the fence confident they had each other's backs. There was another sobering thought; a memorial that greeted the club's patrons as they entered the club. Bill Vowell recalled the memorial this way, "It was a Plexiglas case on a pedestal with a Green Beret and a pair of Sykes—Fairburn commando knives crossed in it. There were three or four names etched on the metal plaques." The year was 1967 and it was late summer. Only a year later Vowell recalled the case "was almost full with the names of those lost/KIA. If you wanted a high risk tour of duty where your chances of coming home in the proverbial body bag were over fifty/fifty, I would have recommended that place hands down."

It was a reminder that F.O.B.s were very vulnerable and not a totally safe place to be. At last the Corporal came to the "hooch" he had been ordered to find. The rumblings coming from inside the stucco walls indicated someone was enjoying a very deserved and deep sleep. This was a special hooch. It served as home to young officers, although only one was currently present. The Corporal craned his neck inside and saw only one cot filled. He approached and carefully aimed his flashlight beam on the name tag. It read Dick, Gamble, Lieutenant. This had to be the place. There was no need to get closer than arm's length. A quick blast from the Corporal's flashlight was followed by a stream of expletives and a "Get that damn light out of my eyes, what the hell is wrong with you?" Apologizing profusely, the Corporal informed the Lieutenant that "They want you in the Tactical Operations Center (T.O.C.) in fifteen minutes." Invoking the magic word "they" gave leverage to the bearer of unwanted news. It was code for people "with higher rank than you sent me, this wasn't my idea." The Lieutenant knew exactly how to decipher the Corporal's cryptic message and he had no intention of holding him personally responsible for the early wake up. Dick also knew that the "Remington Raiders," also known as typists, clerks, office pinks, and "Radar O'Reilly" types hear and see everything that goes on in camp. Before the messenger could reach the door, Dick hit him with the question.

"What's going on?" The Corporal quickly responded that Bruce Baxter's team had been hit hard. A couple of choppers were down and Bruce Baxter and Joseph Kussick, along with some Air Force guys were unaccounted for. The forward air controller had picked up an emergency beeper sound, but no voice contact was made. "They want your Hatchet Force to go and check out the area." With his unofficial briefing completed, the Corporal extinguished his flashlight with the confidence he had successfully completed his mission deep into officer country and had added a new "friend" all in one fell swoop.

Gamble Dick's Hatchet Force had returned only four days previously from a mission just south of the Ashau Valley. The area was considered "Indian country" because neither U.S. nor ARVN (Army of the Republic of Vietnam) artillery could supply the Hatchet Force with a protective umbrella. Each mission was usually followed by some time to decompress, recharge physically and mentally and prepare for the next mission. It was highly unusual to be summoned at zero dark thirty and with only four days rest. It just had a bad feeling to it.

For Lt. Dick there was a positive side to it. He had spent his four days rest preparing his personal gear. Should an emergency occur he would be ready. For this Hatchet Force mission Dick would take the following items:

1. One CAR-15 (rifle—modified M-16)
2. Battle dress uniform (black)
3. 649 rounds of ammo
4. 4 canteens (water)
5. 35 magazines
6. 1 PRC radio
7. Belt and suspender harness
8. Ruck sack
9. 5 canteen pouches
10. Claymore mines (several)
11. Extra radio batteries
12. Grenades
13. C-Rats (not for this 10 hour mission)

Approximately 80 pounds of gear would get you through a mission. Each SOG soldier customized their load to meet personal needs. Many Hatchet Force members used canteen pouches to carry their magazines (7). Each could hold 20 cartridges (bullets), but experience had proven that 20 rounds had weakened the spring causing the rifle to jam. There were no timeouts during a firefight and eighteen rounds proved to be a better match for the M-16. The M-16 had been adopted because of its faster rate of fire and its light weight. Its predecessor had been the M-14, a most reliable and accurate weapon. American soldiers initially dubbed the M-16 the "sand jammer" for its proclivity to malfunction when not kept clean. Better parts and cleaning procedures slowly rescued the rifle's reputation and it is still used by U.S. forces today. The M-16 became another controversy in the American involvement in South East Asia. Had Colt and the U.S. rushed the rifle into the field before it was ready? Had there been any American casualties as a result of the rifle's malfunctioning? In addition, the M-16s did not get into the hands of our South Vietnamese allies until after the 1968 TET Offensive. The M-16 was considered ideally suited for the Vietnam environment. Much of the blame for inadequate numbers of M-16s was laid at the feet of General William Westmoreland who called for the M-16 for American troops in 1965. It is not difficult finding glitches and screw ups in every war, yet Vietnam seemed to have more than its share.

Lt. Dick also kept one pouch filled with tracers only, ". . . it's useful in marking targets for pilots and showing Bulldog's friendly positions. It amounted to the 1960's version of marking targets but without a laser. Two more pouches were dedicated to magazines loaded with 16 rounds of ball ammo (standard bullets) with two rounds of tracer ammo at the bottom." The theory being that the tracers would alert the shooter, it was time to change magazines. These pouches were intended for use should a last ditch effort present itself. "If I began using ammo from these pouches it would be clear that ammo was a critical issue."

Although ammo and water were critical issues and high priority items, there was another piece of equipment both recon teams and Hatchet Forces found absolutely essential, the PRC-25. The "prick 25" radio was an absolute must. Gamble Dick humped his own radio, choosing to forego the luxury of an RTO (radio telephone operator). RTOs were common with regular forces inside Vietnam where English was spoken by everyone. Because the "Indigs" or indigenous forces were used by Special Forces in Cambodia and Laos and composed the bulk of the hatchet and recon teams (they spoke little or no English), they were eliminated from carrying the radio. The remainder of the Americans on each team had their hands full without being tethered to the commander.

Above—North Vietnam's weapon of choice AK-47 supplied by China and the U.S.S.R.

Below—American troops were issued the M-16 ideally suited for jungle warfare.

Sketch by Star Barkman

Each indigenous member of the recon team or Hatchet Force was trained to duplicate the efforts of the Americans on the team. The Indigs learned the Special Forces techniques in the field, but they seldom mastered the English language. In Southeast Asia, the worst case scenario came up occasionally. Laos always seemed to present the worst case scenarios. Trouble could appear in the next landing zone, clearing or anywhere else. The radio was clearly no place for mistakes or indecision. Survival often relied on clear and concise communication with pilots or those back at the F.O.Bs.

For the Hatchet Force members the mission would dictate that the daily hygienic routine would be circumvented so as not to alert NVA trackers and their K-9s to the distinct odors of western soaps, shave cream, shampoo, or toothpaste. That meant that the tiny wool-like sweaters that clung to each tooth would have to remain in place throughout the mission. So too would the salty sweat residue that accumulated even while sleeping. Body odor emanating from each and every orifice must remain. Even the North American diet based on beef might be a dead giveaway to the NVA tracking teams whose diet was based on rice and fish. Although this was the accepted line of thinking in the SOG community, Gamble Dick could not recollect the name of one Special Forces soldier who "would trade a juicy T-bone for a little rice and cold fish." Even SOGs finest had their limitations.

Dick quickly pulled his canvas and leather jungle boots on and methodically wound the boot strings around the boot tops and secured them. When he straightened up, he realized that the three remaining cots in the officer's hooch had not been slept in that night. One of the empty cots would soon be filled by a brand spanking new lieutenant who had yet to arrive, and yet to experience the roller coaster ride he was about to embark on. He was safe, at least for now. The other two cots belonged to Lieutenants Bill Vowell and "Chips" Fleming. Vowell was now considered a skilled and professional Special Forces officer which was somewhat rare. Stranger still, he had never been trained by the Special Forces until he reached Vietnam. He had been trained as a paratrooper in the states and fully expected to serve with the 101st Airborne Division in Vietnam. Although his orders read "SOG," he believed the screw up would be corrected upon reaching Southeast Asia. It never was. For Gamble Dick the Army's snafu (if that's what it was) with the Vowell orders was a God-send. Vowell tutored and mentored Dick in the ways of SOG, staying alive in the initial going was credited to Vowell's willingness to share and teach the "newbie."

Lieutenant Gamble Dick turned out to be just as unique as his name. He was a quick study and described as "one of the bravest of the brave . . . and very smart." He honed both his leadership and survival skills while on the job and that job was "across the fence" and under the most stressful life threatening situations. Those he commanded were the beneficiaries of his talent and courage.

Bill Vowell was currently in Saigon for debriefing on a completed mission that both he and Dick had recently completed. Lt. Dick now found himself in the driver's seat of his very own mission. There would be no Bill Vowell to lean on this time out.

The empty cot belonging to Lt. Chips Fleming presented an entirely different feeling. Fleming had gone with Bruce Baxter and recon team Flatfoot. Flatfoot now found itself engaged with the NVA on Hill 891 in Laos. It was the very place Gamble Dick's Hatchet Force was heading. It could have been the emptiness of the hooch, the extra early wake up or the realization that he would be responsible on this mission. Whatever it was gave Dick an uneasy feeling he would not soon shake.

Forebodings or not, the briefing in the TOC (tactical operations center) would not wait. Dick could take comfort knowing he would be surrounded by the very best NCOs (non-commissioned officers) the United States Army had to offer. The SMM (sergeant majors "mafia") ran the behind the scenes operation for Special Forces. These NCOs had a world of training and experience. Smart young lieutenants took wise counsel from these sergeants, the not-so-smart lieutenants didn't last long.

Dick splashed a little warm canteen water on his face and made a quick visit to the piss tube (it is what it sounds like). The soon to be Hatchet Force commander was now on his way to the most important briefing of his short military career. Even before reaching the TOC, Dick could see far more activity than he had ever seen at 4:00 A.M.; something just wasn't right.

At only 22 years old First Lieutenant Gamble Dick became a quick study in the ways of SOG. Sketch by Star Barkman.

The TOC was "asshole to belly button" with Marine air crews from HMM-263. The outfit was new to this area of operations, having arrived only weeks before. The "jar heads" were milling around the front and left of the TOC. Their heads were moving in a positive up and down manner and an occasional "Wow and Holy Shit" could be heard. The TOC must have looked like the Taj Mahal compared to some of the shit holes the air crews visited. The basic structure was plywood with flat black stenciled letters every four feet that read "Top Secret."

Most of the building materials had been procured from the U.S. Navy Seabees stationed in Phu Bai. They were the construction battalion that won their spurs primarily in the Pacific Theatre throughout World War II. However, one wall was covered with genuine-simulated birch panels. These had been bartered for with genuine-simulated NVA battle flags. The flags had been purchased in Saigon from a local tailor at bulk rates by an enterprising Special Forces Sergeant. They were then dragged through the mud, burned with cigarettes, and finally sprinkled with a liberal dose of chicken blood. The flags were endorsed by a Sergeant as "authentic" and the sergeant often included a brief narrative as to how each flag was taken in hand-to-hand combat. There was no extra charge for the narrative. They went like hot cakes!

The Marine flyboys could not unglue their eyes from the only photograph hanging from the birch paneling. The object of their affection was an 8x10" glossy photo of an ample breasted and leggy creature said to have previously been engaged to a Phu Bai S.F. officer. After only two months in country the officer received a "Dear John'" letter, apparently for her Green Beret to finish his tour was just too painful. She did have two requests: (1) could she keep the engagement ring as a memento, and (2) would he return the nude photo? Being both an officer and a gentleman he complied and sent the negative back to her as a gesture in good faith. He somehow forgot to mention he had reproduced hundreds of flyers and had sent them via helicopter to every fire base in the area. Cynthia's pictures were a huge hit as was the inclusion of her full name, current address and phone number. Legend had it that a flyer found its way into the admiring hands of an NVA officer. It was said that he wrote her a lengthy letter detailing the finest attributes of North Vietnamese's finest. Of course, the gesture by the NVA soldier rendered all hopes of reconciliation impossible.

Master Sergeant Lloyd Fisher had been training seventy-five Cambodian mercenaries for a mission just like the one that was shaping up on Hill 891. Top Sergeant Fisher had already been summoned to the TOC in much the same manner Lieutenant Dick had. He managed to elbow his way through the crowd until he found Lieutenant Dick. Dick wasted no time asking Fisher how long it would take ". . . to get his Red Devil Battalion ready to go?" Sergeant Fisher had bestowed battalion status on his "Bodes" strictly as a gesture. Seventy-five men were less than two platoons, far below the strength of a mighty battalion. Much as expected, Lloyd Fisher indicated they could be ready in minutes if necessary.

In exchange for their soldiering skills SOG reimbursed the mercenaries at a fair rate of pay. Several of the Red Devils sported gold dental work. One even had a star and moon imbedded in his upper front tooth. The practice of using gold as dental material was not unique to "Bodes" operating out of FOB #1. Because the practice was widespread, a rumor circulated that SOG paid their mercenaries with gold. No evidence was ever found that SOG had some method of receiving and disbursing the precious metal, but since SOG was a shadowy organization, the rumor mill continued to grind out the gold story.

The screened door on the TOC violently swung open, nearly coming unhinged, startling the crowd inside, and causing the "jaw jacking" to come to a screeching halt. A large bear disguised as a United States Army Major lumbered up to the plywood podium and slammed his balled up fist on the podium's inclined surface. The podium hopped off the floor, teetered back and forth, and finally settled down.

Major Ira Snell was the camp commander. He was also of African-American descent making him a rarity and pioneer of sorts as a field grade officer in Special Forces. It appeared he had spent half his life in a weight training room and the other half on the collegiate gridiron where he played varsity football at North Carolina A&T. His lower jaw preceded the rest of him by eighteen inches and he had a carotid artery with the diameter of a garden hose. He made famed tough guy, NFL coach and philosopher, Vince Lombardi, look tame. The major quickly turned his wrath on the Marine pilots with an icy stare that must have sent them back to their training days at Quantico, Virginia. The Marines responded as if a rifle cleaning rod had been jammed up their anal passage which undoubtedly was the effect the Major intended. On at least one occasion he had offered to remove his oak leaves and do battle with an N.C.O. The Sergeant declined the invitation. One thing was certain, Snell had very little time in the field as a source for leadership experience. His physical presence and demeanor would have to do along with his combative attitude.

Speaking in a raspy voice, Snell began his message. "Everything you see, hear, smell, touch or taste here and that includes the coffee, is classified. Top Secret! Does everyone understand that?" This, of course, was a rhetorical question. No answer was expected and none were offered. "Any breach of security will be dealt with quickly and severely. Everybody OK with that? Anybody wanting to leave, leave now and nothing will ever be said, everyone understand?" A pause followed with some hushed murmurs and heads that moved like bobble head dolls. "Good" said the Major, cutting the pause off abruptly. Snell may not have accrued much time on missions, but he was pretty skilled inside the tactical operations centers. He knew full well that a Marine, be it air wing, grunt, or office pink, could not return to their superior officers with tail between their legs. It would not look good. Unbeknownst to the Marine pilots, they had signed on to fly a SOG Hatchet Force into Laos, a neutral country that concealed a sizeable portion of the Ho Chi Minh Trail. Everywhere they were about to go was technically denied territory to U.S. ground troops.

Major Snell's captive audience quickly felt the urgency of what was unfolding and all eyes followed him to a map stand to the right of the podium. Snell flipped a piece of limp canvas over the back of the map stand, exposing a map showing northern South Vietnam, eastern Laos, the DMZ (demilitarized zone) and southern North Vietnam. The crowd edged forward collectively trying to get a view of where their mission would take them. The pucker factor (sphincter contraction) was beginning to take effect. One look at this area even impressed veteran Special Forces Sergeant Lloyd Fisher of the seriousness of the mission. Scanning the crowd, Snell began by saying, "You are currently in a SOG camp. It stands for studies and observation group. Our mission here is to monitor the Ho Chi Minh Trail, rescue downed pilots, amongst other things." Snell slapped the rubber tipped wooden pointer on the map to what appeared to be a trail labeled B-45. B-45 connected the Ashau Valley to the Ho Chi Minh Trail. Snell used it as a point of reference as it was well known to SOG as a very active and dangerous area. With a second tap of his pointer he raised his voice and said, "Here, this is where we inserted recon team Flatfoot. We inserted them eighteen kilometers inside of Laos. They ran into trouble last evening. Try as they may they could not shake a very strong and persistent NVA effort to eliminate them." Snell continued. He included what little confirmed information there was on the rescue effort to date. One part of his laundry list of information was most troubling and that was the NVA's success in downing three helicopters attempting to rescue recon team Flatfoot. One was a South Vietnamese Kingbee, the second was a U.S. Army Huey Slick and the last was an Air Force Jolly Green Giant. It was an unusual number of helos to lose and lead the S.F. men to believe a well trained and supplied NVA awaited.

Snell concluded, "It's a mess on 891 and come first light we are going to clean it up." A somewhat inexperienced Gamble Dick still was able to recognize a lack of specificity in Snell's presentation and the three missing helos and unknown status of their crews was real reason for concern. Some solace could be taken in Snell's direct approach and the positive spin he used in concluding his remarks.

The remainder of the briefing was handled by Captain Billy R. Davis who lacked Snell's flare for dramatics or imposing physical presence. Captain Davis had arrived at FOB #1 Phu Bai as the OIC (officer in charge) of A-323, a Special Forces team on loan from Okinawa. Upon arrival Davis had landed the job of camp operations officer. The position prevented him from venturing across the fence into Indian Territory with the rest of his team. By default, Lieutenant Hoepner had inherited the reins of team A-323. A powerful physical specimen, Hoepner spent more time on missions than most officers. His home was Walla Walla, Washington. Lieutenant Hoepner could command the Hatchet Force; however, Lieutenant Dick was senior to Hoepner and that became the deciding factor as to who would lead the rescue/recovery.

Hatchet Forces were inherently more conventional than recon teams but still less conventional than regular army infantry units. Command of the Hatchet Force would be in the hands of Lieutenant Gamble Dick. As practiced by SOG when an officer accompanied a team, be it reconnaissance or Hatchet Force, the officer became responsible for the overall organization, the planning, the transportation, and blame if things should go south (and at times they would). The actual leadership of the men fell under the auspices of the senior NCO (Sergeant). The mission to Hill 891 had no shortage of successful NCOs. Lloyd Fisher was the obvious choice and no one could recommend anyone more respected or experienced. The division of leadership under these missions seemed to be a loose fit yet the SOG teams made it work.

Captain Davis added what small amount of intel that had been made available and Major Snell had bequeathed to him. He did add an interesting item when he included the terms "flak trap" in his presentation. The NVA developed a tactic that used a surrounded SOG team or downed helicopter crew as bait. Knowing that air assets would be used to rescue their fellow Americans the NVA would concentrate as many troops as were available and bring up the heaviest guns they could. The NVA would keep pressure on the bait in hopes of downing the rescuers. United States Air

Force Major Jimmy Kilbourne subscribed to the "flak trap" theory. He also authored a paper regarding it. He flew his A1-E Skyraider over Hill 891 and drew the attention of the NVA gunners who did everything they possibly could to ruin the Major's mission and bring about his early demise. The A1-Es and their pilots were totally despised by the NVA because of their effective and devastating delivery of ordinance versus ground troops.

The NVA had already accounted for two crashed helicopters: The two badly damaged helos, Major Kilborne's shot up Skyraider and more importantly sixteen men were unaccounted for; four Air Force crewmen, four Army crewmen, five recon team members and three VNAF crewmen. Major Snell may not have been privy to much "intel" but he was dead right about one thing—it was a mess! It was unlikely the mess was going away on its own. The NVA might even strengthen its hold on Hill 891. They were not going to allow Americans to just walk off the mountainside before inflicting more casualties or bringing down more aircraft. For the time being Uncle Ho's nephews had things going pretty much the way they wanted. That was about to change.

The Hatchet Force was given the call sign (for radio purposes) "Bulldog" by the signal operating instructor. Planning and organizing was immediately initiated by Lieutenants Dick and Hoepner under the guidance of top Sergeant Lloyd Fisher who kept a watchful eye on the less experienced officers.

The lead officers and N.C.O.s had been advised by Rescue Control Center-Saigon through Captain Davis that rescue beepers had been activated on the mountainside. The question was by whom? Was it the good guys or had the NVA procured the rescue beeper devices? Both the A-1Es and Covey pilots had reported hearing the signal device air crews could activate should they require rescue. It was possible to use a voice to communicate to rescuers, although this was not reported to be the case throughout the search and rescue operation on Hill 891.

The beeper's only signal raised concern that the rescue device may have fallen into the hands of the NVA and was being used to lure in rescue aircraft so they could be shot down. The beepers were reported in operation throughout the search and rescue mission and were cause for a cautious approach by pilots and the Hatchet Force.

Maps were distributed to Bulldog's team leaders, as it had been determined that the Hatchet Force would be inserted several thousand meters from the crash site. Bulldog was also informed that their mission would not exceed a total of ten hours and would not be conducted during the dark hours. This information allowed Bulldog to hump less weight and leave excess equipment back at camp. Such things as food, entrenching tools, night defensive ordnance and even a certain quantity of water could be left in the rear. Daylight operations always seemed safer. It removed one element of difficulty and made air power more available.

Bulldog's medic, Ron Bock, recalled his conversation with Lieutenant Rod Hoepner concerning the mission. "Hoepner said that we were just going to take a quick look see, to travel light and no ruck sack, just pistol belt with ammo and canteens. He said that we would be on the ground only a very short time and anything other than basic pistol belt equipment would be unnecessary and only slow us down. Presumably this quick recon would be followed by a more substantial mission if so indicated."

Besides the information passed on to Bulldog's leaders, they were issued formal orders. You will work your way to the crash site, determine the fate of the helicopters and personnel, and deal with the situation accordingly. "Deal with the situation accordingly?" This statement certainly left a lot to the hatchet force leaders to determine. You will remove any sensitive material and get out. Enemy prisoners should be taken, as should their equipment. Chances of heavy contact with NVA forces were deemed to be very probable. No further reconnaissance would be done and it was unlikely more details would become available before the Hatchet Force would board the helos destined for Hill 891 inside of Laos.

Weather, always problematic in the mountains, was not discussed. SOG teams relied heavily on helicopters for transportation and the helos were often made available subject to the ever changing Laotian weather patterns. Missions ordered and planning had to be kept fluid and SOG teams were very adept at working with weather-related constraints.

Whether it was the early wake up, Major Snell's Knute Rockne portrayal, lack of specifics or the lack of preparation and planning, Gamble Dick had to fight off the negative thoughts that dogged his mental preparation. There was, however, one very positive element to be found regarding Bulldog's mission (besides the 8 x 10 glossy) and that was the world of experience Master Sergeant Lloyd Fisher brought to the rescue mission. A professional in every sense of the word, he possessed a rare combination of skills and personality traits. Some of his many gifts may have been on loan from God, some he had developed and honed on his own and the remainder can be attributed to his Special Forces training. He had won over both the hearts and minds of those he served with and trained. He seldom raised his voice and always kept his verbal communications to a minimum. Fisher's calm demeanor was contagious and even during the hairiest of engagements he was able to manage his emotions.

Team A-323 was on temporary duty at F.O.B. 1. Eight of the team went on the mission to Hill 891. Front Row-L to R—*Sp. 5 Rick Bayer, *2nd Lt. Rod Hoepner, *SFC. Erkine Osborne, Sgt. Phil Quinn, *Sgt. Ron Bock, *SFC Bruce Lutrell. Back Row—L to R—*SFC Gilbert Hamilton, *SFC Brooke Bell, *MSgt. Lloyd Fisher, Capt. Billy Davis, SFC Jim Scurry, SFC Earl Kalani.

*Participated on the mission. Photo courtesy of Ron Bock.

Special Forces Master Sergeant Lloyd Fisher seemed to be a natural at leading men and applying both his talent and skills. Sketch by Star Barkman.

Former Special Forces Sergeant Bob Cavanaugh once went on a reconnaissance mission with Lloyd Fisher near the Ia Drang Valley. The small recon team had been inserted in the middle of a large concentration of NVA soldiers. At one point the Special Forces team was so close to the NVA that they had to lie down in the undergrowth where they actually could smell the NVA walking past. Fisher had taken refuge behind Cavanaugh and observed Cavanaugh's leg nervously move up and down repeatedly until danger passed. Once on their feet, Fisher questioned Cavanaugh about the stinging ants until he had extracted a confession that there weren't any ants. "I was just scared shitless." Fisher just seemed to be made for trying situations and even found humor in them.

Master Sergeant Fisher's laid back style of leadership was not to be taken as a sign of weakness. Unlike the stereotype NCO (sergeants) who relied on bellicose and profanity laced tirades to achieve results from the lower rank enlisted men, Fisher was a true trainer and leader.

On one mission to rescue or recover recon team Indiana, a Marine helo showed up to extract the Hatchet Force Fisher was working with. As the helos moved in, one of the Marine crewmen was killed when the helo was hosed down by an NVA machine gun. Undaunted, the rest of the helicopters made it into the landing zone and took on the besieged Hatchet Force. Now working with one fewer helo, the extra weight became a factor. When the chopper Fisher's group embarked on failed to lift off, the crew chief nudged one of the Cambodian mercenaries out the door. An American Special Forces guy quickly jumped from the helo to ensure the helo would return.

Top Fisher realized the Special Forces guy was Lieutenant Dick, and during the flight back to Phu Bai he dropped in on the pilot just to make sure he intended to make a return trip. The pilot and co-pilot felt that it was getting too near to dark and felt first light would be the best time to make a return trip. Fisher knew Lieutenant Dick and the Cambodian could not hold off the NVA all night and by morning there would only be bodies to recover. Fisher quickly stuffed his .45 Colt in the pilot's face and was promised an immediate return trip which Fisher personally supervised. Both men were recovered, but not without further close calls. Years later, Fisher admitted to Dick that he had interceded on Dick's behalf, but when asked if he had threatened anyone with a weapon he only admitted that "I took care of it."

Sergeant First Class Robert Cavanaugh served with Lloyd Fisher several times and purely by chance went along on the mission to Hill 891 solely out of respect for Fisher. Cavanaugh and Fisher played handball hundreds of times as part of their physical training and fitness. Cavanaugh never bested Fisher in their long series of rivalries. On one occasion, Fisher had contracted flu-like symptoms and looked like an easy mark for Cavanaugh, but once again Fisher won. It's the only grudge to this day Cavanaugh holds against his old friend. Special Forces would have done well to harvest some of Fisher's DNA for cloning purposes. One NCO thought Fisher should have been an officer, a high ranking officer.

Bulldog also found experience and leadership in First Sergeant Bruce Lutrell whose specialty was intelligence and whose personality differed greatly from Fisher's. Lutrell was somewhat of a type A personality. He had a slight edge to him and an aggressive style in the field. He was an effective leader in his own right. Good teams often had differing styles and personalities, yet they were able to complement one another and utilize individual strengths. It was also said that Lutrell possessed the heart of a warrior along with the ability to find humor in the inevitable snafus that often frustrated military professionals. Bulldog was indeed fortunate to have two very experienced leaders to lean on for this mission. Sadly, during his second tour of duty with 5th Special Forces, Bruce Lutrell was killed in action. Unlike draftees, Special Forces professionals often performed multiple tours of duty. Their over-exposure to the most hazardous situations quite often ended their lives.

Hatchet Force Bulldog went to Hill 891 with one weapons expert in the person of Brook Bell. Always cooperative with the men (NCOs) it was officers he chose to avoid. No one really knew how Bell developed his bad attitude toward officers. It may have been he just didn't like taking orders, although the Army would be a strange place to be if that were the case. Special Forces had long been a refuge for NCOs and officers seldom found their careers heading upwards while stuck in Special Forces. Special Forces may have been the best fit for Bell, as it appealed to those who didn't quite fit into the regular Army. That aside, Bell was a very competent and solid Special Forces sergeant who would not back down in difficult situations. Besides, he was an expert with an M-60 machine gun as the NVA would soon find out.

Bulldog also included two demolition experts, Erskine Osborne (a.k.a. Ozzy) and Specialist 5 Alrich (Rick) Bayer. Osborn's mission to Hill 891 was short lived when misfortune struck early on. Rick Bayer was a completely different story. He was an outstanding field soldier and a team man all the way. When not in the field, he often walked a bit on the wild side. He never met an officer he liked and that included Gamble Dick. Even top Fisher referred to Rick as a "little mischievous" and Fisher was famous for understating. Fisher often played a shell game with Rick, moving him around, running interference for him and keeping him just out of officer's reach. In a way Fisher had an unspoken arrangement with the officers. They allowed him a lot of latitude when it came to personnel decisions. This was not totally unique to SOG operations. Fisher was unimpressed with shiny boots and belt buckles, neither snappy salutes nor close shaves helped to win firefights in the jungle.

There were two medics assigned to the team, Sergeant First Class Jim Scurry and Sergeant Ronald "Doc" Bock. Scurry was a man among men. He had a reputation for fearlessness and whether he just refused to acknowledge fear, or just plain disregarded it, no one knew for sure. A man for all seasons, Scurry was a top flight medic who possessed both the qualities of toughness along with a gentle and kind way, especially with his patients. It was surely Bulldog's loss when Scurry became unavailable for the mission to Hill 891.

That would leave Ron Bock as the lone medic to make the mission to Hill 891 in Laos. Bulldog would be a large contingent for only one medic and Bock would have to rely on the cross training the Special Forces provided for each of their soldiers to augment his own considerable skills. By all accounts Ron Bock was a serious student of field medicine, and his thoughtful and kind gestures only added to his character. Another side of Bock would surface on Hill 891, a side that would be remembered and live in the hearts of his fellow countrymen.

The final two Special Forces members of Bulldog were Sergeant Gary Spann and S.F.C. Gilbert Hamilton, or "Hambone," as he was known to the men. Hambone was admired for his can-do attitude and fierce warrior mentality that at times went just beyond being brave. Then Lieutenant Bill Vowell assessed Hamilton in this way, "He took unnecessary chances and was a very brave soldier whose bravery would not see him through his tour alive." Like several of his fellow NCOs, Hamilton was not a huge fan of officers. Although the officers admired him, he kept them at a distance. Hamilton would play a large role in Bulldog's mission to rescue and recover on Hill 891. Fate would not be kind to Spann and Hamilton. Less than a month after surviving Hill 891 they both were wounded in action on yet another hill in Laos. Hamilton succumbed to his wound several weeks later. They were credited with saving the lives of their remaining team members. One of the lives saved belonged to Lieutenant Gamble Dick who commented that, "it broke my heart and not a day goes by I don't think about them . . ." Irony is a worn out word, yet it is the only way to describe Gilbert Hamilton's willingness to give up his life for an officer.

SOG teams had to overcome varied personalities, injuries, sickness, misfortune and even the death of fellow team members. Hardships were common to nearly all SOG teams. It was a given that each individual dealt with losses and moved on. Each team persevered and overcame great odds, more often than not. Bulldog now had to "cross the fence and stomp on the tiger's balls," hopefully return and then prepare to do it all over again.

CHAPTER 9

NICE DOGGY

Landing Zone, F.O.B. #1 Phu Bai, SVN, 0900 hours, 9 November, 1967

How dangerous was Hatchet Force Bulldog's mission going to be? It only took a quick count of the nearly seventy-five members composing the effort to answer the question. This was a huge operation by SOG standards. Someone somewhere was mighty anxious to bring an end to the disaster that continued to multiply on Hill 891. The expression "shit rolls downhill" is used in the military to describe graphically how orders originate at the top of the chain but are carried out somewhere down the line. It was no wonder Major Snell's carotid artery was pulsating out of control. The order to clean up the mess likely originated at CINCPAC (commander in Chief of Pacific forces). For Snell, the pressure may have been ratcheted up with the knowledge that the White House was being kept apprised of the situation.

Seventy-five armed men for a Hatchet Force might have given the uninitiated cause to feel some comfort, but senior NCO Lloyd Fisher was less than comfortable. He knew Hill 891 would be a challenging ten hours, even with seventy-five men.

The landing zone at Forward Operating Base Phu Bai began to fill up with Cambodian mercenaries and the American Special Forces soldiers. Packs and rifles were bunched in clusters off to the side of the landing zone and the orange glow of cigarette ash dotted the darkness. The wait for the full compliment of helos to arrive had begun. Coordinating helicopters supplied by the South Vietnamese Air Force and the

United States Marine Corps would prove to be a challenge. The South Vietnamese flew American hand-me-downs and the Marines had their own operations to worry about. The Cambodians took up their normal squatting positions and the Americans congregated in two's and three's undoubtedly cursing the waiting game that heightened the anxiety they already felt.

The talking, milling, and normal grab ass soon came to a halt when the waiting men caught a glimpse of two silhouettes striding towards the LZ. The morning mist and darkness swirled around them and obscured their faces. It appeared as if only uniforms were walking as they closed in on the LZ. Their size and stride made them Americans but they weren't from F.O.B. #1. All the Special Forces guys assigned to Bulldog were already present. They walked two abreast, like something out of a Wyatt Earp western. As they closed on the Hatchet Force a name could be put on one familiar face. It was Master Sergeant Charles "Skip" Minnicks.

There were SOG men and there were legendary SOG men. Skip was a member of the latter group. He was a superior woodsman and trainer of Special Forces techniques. Some say he was a natural in the ways of counter insurgency. He had a hulking frame with the finesse and agility of an apex predator. Word had it he was of Native American descent. On this day he teamed with Sergeant First Class Robert Cavanaugh who already had an impressive resume in the Special Forces and was now honing his considerable skills under Minnick's watchful eye. At some point the most promising first sergeants would fill the rather large shoes of the masters such as Minnicks and Fisher, now 38 and 37 years old respectively. At some later point the student would take on legendary proportions just like their tutors.

No one can recall missions and names of SOG men like the legendary Billy Waugh. "I worked with American Recon men Charles Jenkins and "Skip" Minnicks (our best POW snatchers) who ordered an H-34 "Kingbee" to land among a group of hoochs along the Ho Chi Minh Trail in broad daylight. They kicked the door in and dragged out an NVA and the NVA's weapon threw him on the helicopter and flew away with the newly acquired POW displaying gonads, not the size of bowling balls, the size of medicine balls!"

SOG legend "Skip" Minnicks (right) barbeques some ribs between missions. Photo courtesy of Bob Cavanaugh.

Minnicks and Cavanaugh had just completed a debriefing in Saigon following their latest mission. Their transportation left them at Phu Bai for the night. The following day they would return to F.O.B. #4 in Khe Sanh. When the two found out that Bruce Baxter's recon team was in trouble they decided to "lend a hand." Besides both knew Lloyd Fisher. Having drawn ammo from the Phu Bai armorer, both Cavanaugh and Minnicks were already renewing old friendships and listening to what was taking place on Hill 891. The act of adding two men to the already established mix was pretty much unheard of within traditional units. It was a totally accepted practice to SOG, so much so that Skip Minnicks did not seek approval from his own base, nor did he even leave a message at F.O.B. #4. They assumed it was OK and they did it. The addition of another experienced N.C.O. like Skip Minnicks would not ruffle the feathers of young lieutenants like Dick and Hoepner, but bruised egos were much preferred to getting team members or you killed. Lloyd Fisher and Skip Minnicks provided a safety net for less experienced officers who viewed the experienced N.C.O.s as a positive, and besides it was the way things were done by SOG.

Time passed slowly for the Hatchet Force awaiting their transportation. The anticipation and initial adrenaline injection began to lose its edge. Waiting for the unknown was tough on the psyche, but now the Southeast Asian heat and humidity began to build. The spilled hydraulic oil and aviation fuel comingled, providing a nauseating odor. Coupled with humidity, heat, and dust, the men began to empty their canteens in an effort to remain hydrated.

Heat casualties often played a negative role in the performance of combat teams in Southeast Asia. It was always advisable to consume as much water as possible. However, drinking too much water could leave the Hatchet Force with nothing to drink on their mission. There was no intelligence that water could be found on Hill 891, and if it existed, was it potable?

Several hours passed since Bulldog's men had formed up at the LZ. Finally the Corporal double timed through the thoroughly pissed off men and cautiously approached Gamble Dick. It was the same Corporal who had awakened the Lieutenant earlier and used the very same phrase, "They (higher ranking officers) sent him to inform Bulldog to stand down (delay) temporarily and return to their quarters."

The word was passed to stand down and the Cambodians began to scurry around to refill their depleted canteens and find some shade to rest in. They immediately clustered up and began conversing among themselves in what sounded like jabberwocky, but what probably amounted to bitching and griping about the wait and the incompetent leadership that lead to yet another snafu (situation normal, all fucked up). This was an age old tradition practiced by all soldiers since there were armies and officers to run the armies.

Bulldog's leaders, both officers and senior N.C.O.s, made their way to the T.O.C. (tactical operations center) to receive any updates on the situation that recon team Flatfoot was embroiled in. There was very little news regarding Flatfoot, however, they learned the hold up was due to the lack of helos. No one was surprised. There always seemed to be too many missions and too few choppers. This time the Marine helos assigned to Bulldog first had to drop a battalion off just west of Hue along Highway #1 for one of their famous security sweeps. French troops had coined the phrase "La Rue Sans Joie" while trying to maintain France's hold on Vietnam. It was on this little avenue to heaven where the French moved war materiel that they became acquainted with the Viet Minh, a first cousin to the Viet Cong (Charlie), who were now entrusted with disrupting Americans transporting their war materiel.

The constant battle for the control of Highway #1 served as inspiration for Bernard Fall's book entitled <u>Street Without Joy</u>. In it, Fall became a modern day Nostradamus by questioning whether the American mindset and culture could adapt to the Viet Cong's insurgent tactics. So enthralling did Fall find La Rue Sans Joie that he lost his own life in 1967 to a V.C. land mine while monitoring a U.S.M.C. sweep not far from Hue. The V.C. (Viet Cong) and the U.S.M.C. both utilized the road. Needless to say, neither was comfortable with the other. Sometimes the sweeps turned out to be just a walk in the sun, albeit the very hot sun. At other times, the V.C. sprung ambushes or left booby traps that caused some horrendous injuries to the Marine "grunts". Because the VC were elusive and seldom stood their ground, the Marines were often frustrated that when they did catch up to "Charlie" (the VC) they were treated like target practice.

The 6 Ps
"Prior Planning Prevents Piss Poor Performance"

The visit to the T.O.C. provided nothing regarding the events unfolding on Hill 891. However, it was revealed that fourteen helicopters would be used to insert Bulldog into Laos. Eight helos would be provided by the VNAF and six additional helos would come from the Marines H-MM-263. Two chase helicopters would follow the troop bearing ships in case of mechanical failure or a shoot down. The landing zone for Bulldog would be east northeast of recon team Flatfoot's current position and that of the Jolly Green crash site. It was possible more information would be made available prior to the Hatchet Forces departure, although this scenario never materialized. As it turned out, specifics such as who was unaccounted for, how many helicopters were down, enemy numbers on Hill 891, and the type of weapons used by the NVA never became available to Bulldog.

Former Special Forces Sergeant First Class Ron Bock assessed the planning this way, "The senior NCOs were very experienced and professional soldiers who exercised responsible, individual initiative. They were used to responding to emergencies at a moment's notice. After all, Hatchet Forces were to be quick response teams that rarely had the time for careful preparation. The recovery team of about 45 Cambodians and 15 Americans was armed with two M-60 machine guns, a BAR (Browning automatic rifle) World War II era, an M-79 grenade launcher, a Claymore-mine, M-16s and CAR-15 rifles and hand grenades. The senior NCOs had insured the team was well armed."

The Hatchet Force was assigned call sign "Bulldog". At 75 men strong it was hoped to have the bite of it's namesake. Sketch by Star Barkman.

Bulldog's plan would have to be simplified and basic. Although much had transpired on the side of the Laotian mountain, very few facts had made it back to Phu Bai. The fate of the VNAF Kingbee that had been shot up and limped off the mountainside was unknown until the entire operation was completed. Likewise, the Army helo piloted by Kent Woolridge and William Zanow was said to have crashed, but this was yet to be confirmed. It had also been assumed that the entire crew from the Jolly Green had perished on the face of the mountainside. Flatfoot's status was still totally unclear. This lack of clarity hampered Bulldog's rescue effort from the very start of the mission until they were extracted. One thing was very clear: the mission would be a very dangerous and challenging ten hours.

Bulldog's senior N.C.O.s and officers quickly departed the T.O.C., having little to show for the time invested. They turned their attention to filling their own canteens and rechecking their personal gear. Lieutenant Dick returned to the officer's hooch and rummaged through an open case of C-rations. What he stumbled on was a real prize—an olive drab can stamped "peaches" on the top. It was a real find. The peaches were always ripe and they were drenched in thick, sweet syrup. Along with the fruit cocktail and pears, this was a real culinary delight. Peaches could be traded for the most sought after cigarettes, Winstons or Marlboros. You could even barter them for toilet paper. The peaches didn't weigh much and fit easily into your pack or cargo pocket. It would be a perfect snack for a ten hour mission. No sooner had the peaches been stored than that same Corporal poked his head in the door and advised that Bulldog needed to double time to the L.Z. The Choppers were inbound.

L.Z. F.O.B. #1 Phu Bai, SVN, 0945 hours, 9 November, 1967

Once again Master Sergeant Lloyd Fisher had his Red Devils (Cambodians) organized and ready to embark the helicopters. This time they could actually hear the incoming helos which had refueled at Phu Bai and making their approach. The VNAF helicopters swooped in, and when they did, a blizzard of oil contaminated dust swept through the L.Z. The sweaty faces of the Hatchet Force became a magnet to the dust, dirt and small particles of vegetation. The sticky mess seeped between their shoulder blades and ran down their chests. It settled on eyelids and between fingers. Some of the air born goo had to have been inhaled. It wormed its way beneath their waistbands and continued further south. The filth went along with the job, and every Special Forces soldier had endured it for a lot longer than ten hours. To them it was barely worth mentioning.

Of greater concern was the effect the grit would have on the operation of the weapons, sifting into the barrels, and worse, into the "action" (moving parts) of the rifles. They might jam and fail to eject spent casings. On board a helicopter was no place to be performing a cursory cleaning of one's weapon. Hopefully, the landing zone would be cold, and time would permit for a brief rifle maintenance session after clearing the L.Z.

The first of the VNAF Kingbee helicopters touched down and five men scrambled on board. Lieutenant Dick was the last man on the fist chopper out. His boots would be the first to hit the ground when the Kingbee touched down on Laotian soil. As the final of the eight Kingbees lifted off, the Marine H-34s touched down, swallowed their share of Hatchet Force Bulldog and joined the Kingbees on their way into Laos. The embarkation was textbook and the departure was flawless.

The jungle below passed in varying shades of green almost as if it were an ocean. Never once did the triple canopy trees betray what lay hidden below on the jungle floor. At one point the helos cruised over the Ashau Valley, dubbed "The Valley of Death", probably named by some "straight leg" (infantryman) that had a close call there or lost a buddy to the NVA that frequented the area. Not long after the Valley flyover, the pilots began to gain altitude when the Truong Son Mountains came into view. Flying at five thousand feet A.G.L. (above ground level), the air thinned out and provided a natural air-conditioning. The cooling effect would be Bulldog's last taste of comfort for some time.

A thin wisp of smoke drifted straight up from a mountainside. It was Hill 891 and when the crew chief saw it he tugged at Lieutenant Dick's sleeve. He pointed northeast and said "L.Z." Dick pulled a map out of his shirt, oriented it, and quickly returned it inside his shirt. The smoke was most likely a helicopter burning and the whitish color may have indicated aluminum or magnesium was the fuel. Both were used in the construction of helicopters. It was likely men had already died and any that hadn't were struggling to remain alive. The NVA was currently king of the mountain and they would surely kill anyone who would try to dislodge them. An unsettled feeling engulfed the men. Unknown and unanswered questions teased their minds.

All 16 choppers remained at a high altitude not wanting to fall prey to the NVA gunners who already claimed 3 helos to their credit. Once over the L.Z. the lead VNAF pilot sent his Kingbee into a death spiral, corkscrewing his aircraft closer and closer to the ground. It felt as if the bottom dropped out and your Adam's apple was shaking hands with your lower gastro region. Dick called it the "E ticket ride". He claimed it to be the ultimate high and still feels Walt Disney's ride engineers are missing out on a great attraction. Centrifugal force pinned the team members to the floor of the ancient Kingbee as if super glue had been applied to their boot bottoms and ass cheeks. The grip is not released until the pilot flares the ship (halts downward motion) and the skids touched terra terra firma. The VNAF pilots had two histories: first as the bravest and most competent pilots in Southeast Asia and following 1968-69 as much less effective pilots. By that time the best pilots had been killed and their replacements as a whole were not of the same quality, having been sent to flight training for less time and sometimes promoted by corrupt friends.

Two Marine pilots recalled the mission to insert Bulldog. One was Captain Paul Gregoire and the other was Captain Joe Hanner. Gregoire recalled the briefing by Major Snell and finding out that the helos destination was Laos, "That mysterious place to the west that was always spoken of with dread. It was Indian country at its' worst; a forbidding place crawling with large numbers of North Vietnamese armed with huge numbers of heavy anti-aircraft guns." That information was largely obtained not from intelligence reports but from stories told at bars. As it turned out, the rumors from half in the bag Marines had a high degree of accuracy.

Captain Joe Hanner recalled Mitch Gibbs as his crew chief on the way out. His log books also revealed that all extra weight on the helo had been removed by Gibbs and that the gunner was also left behind. Extra machine gun ammo was the only luxury item taken. The L.Z. turned out to be cold and on the return to Phu Bai Gregoire allowed himself a cigarette from a fresh pack. He had already gone through one entire pack and figured he would exhaust a second before getting some rack time.

The extract on November 11th drew some small arms fire. One NVA opened up with what Gregoire identified as a 12.7 MM machine gun. The U.S. Air Force quickly pounced on the gun and it went silent. Gregoire concluded that "The close air support had done the job." Captain Hanner noted that he was 28 ½ minutes into the 30 minute low fuel light when he returned from the extract.

The helos quickly regurgitated the contents of their passenger compartments onto the floor of the L.Z. The men exited crouching and bent over to avoid the lethal rotors overhead and also as a result of the weight of their packs. Lieutenant Dick's contingent scrambled to face the area deemed most likely to produce an NVA ambush. Each succeeding helo's men exited and formed a 360º circle around the L.Z.

Landing Vicinity Y, Laos, 1030 hours, 9 November, 1967

Getting into an L.Z. is a very treacherous time for a hatchet force or a recon team; not to mention the inviting target a helicopter makes. There was no fight to be had at the L.Z.; it was stone cold. The enemy had probably set up an ambush on another possible L.Z. site. They couldn't cover them all, and they guessed wrong this time. Bulldog was off to a very good start as the helicopters disappeared and turned into black bobbing dots in just a few moments.

The Hatchet Force was now alone in Uncle Ho's neighborhood far behind enemy lines. The force that had looked so bad and robust back at Phu Bai seemed much less formidable in the field. The L.Z. was no place to loiter. 16 helicopters had made a lot of noise and dust. How many NVA eyes had witnessed their arrival?

Lieutenant Dick wasted no time contacting the FAC (forward air controller) who was prowling over Hill 891 in his 02 Cessna Skymaster. At this juncture in the mission the Cessna was piloted by Air Force Captain Corwin "Kip" Kippenhan. Dick's message was brief, "Hatchet Force Bulldog is leaving for the crash site immediately." The FAC pilot "Rogered your last, Force leaving for crash site." The Cessna then swung out in a long loop so as not to give Bulldog's position away. Kippenhan would soon bring his aircraft back over the Hatchet Force and repeat this over and over. Kippenhan had a passenger on this trip. Sitting to his right was Sergeant First Class Dudley Nutter, a Special Forces soldier attached to SOG. His job was to aide the pilot in deciphering what the recon team or Hatchet Force below really needed to stay alive and complete a mission successfully. The position Sergeant Nutter was filling was widely known as a "Covey Rider."

The Captain and Sergeant had flown together before and appreciated each other's company. They were, of course, the odd couple as highly educated officers rarely worked alongside a less polished Army enlisted man. SOG was far more interested in results than maintaining military protocol. The FAC pilots were warriors and had little regard for protocol. Several days prior to the mission on Hill 891 the odd couple had been sent on another mission. Flying out of Da Nang, Nutter quickly dozed off and did not respond to Kippenhan's conversation. Usually a serious and straight laced officer, Kippenhan devised a perfect wake up call for his right seater. Waiting until his Skymaster had left the city lights far behind, he sent the Cessna into a barrel roll. Startled and awakened while upside down and hanging from his harness, Nutter sensed something had gone horribly wrong. Screaming, "What the fuck is going on?" he quickly caught a slight grin on Kippenhan's face and realized it was all nothing but a ruse. Needless to say, Nutter never drifted off in the cockpit again.

Corwin Kippenhan had previously flown misty FACS up north. "Misty" was the call sign for forward air controllers who flew "fast movers" or jets so far north that they could see Hanoi's city lights. Misty FACs were used there because the North Vietnamese had been treated by the Chinese to some very sophisticated anti-aircraft equipment. Early one evening Captain Kippenhan's luck ran out when his jet was hit by anti-aircraft fire forcing him to bail out and spend a terrifying night in Hanoi's backyard.

Kippenhan was rescued and sent to train in 02 Cessnas. After 10 days of training he was sent to fly the less glamorous, but no less dangerous, prop driven aircraft in support of SOG operations in Laos. Throughout the days prior to and following November 8th Kippenhan had waged a personal battle with a bad case of stomach cramps along with all the other unpleasant bodily malfunctions. There were never enough FAC flyers to support the SOG missions which forced the constant use of the same pilots over and over again. The bond that was formed among the pilots and the recon and hatchet teams became a strong one. When recon teams were lost to superior NVA forces, the pilots took it personally. It affected their morale. At one point Kippenhan felt the dysentery he experienced was actually a loss of nerve. Yet he continued to fly his missions and support the Special Forces missions and men he had grown to admire and who admired his considerable skills. Towards the end of his tour Kippenhan's support for the war had been damaged. It saddened him greatly to see the SOG teams suffer losses that were unacceptable and quite predictable. Referring to them as suicide missions, Kippenhan failed to see how losses of SOG lives were worthwhile to the big picture.

Kippenhan, Covey 57, and several others would handle the entire mess on Hill 891. One would relieve the other and manage to bring order where chaos seemed to reign supreme. Covey 57 had helped Jack McTasney and his Jolly Green escape the mountainside and his calm, cool professionalism was totally required. To characterize the Covey fliers as unsung heroes would be a total injustice to them. The incredible responsibility they shouldered managing the wildest situations was the stuff of courage and heroism. They were the glue that kept men alive and kept helos and airplanes from disaster, albeit by the narrowest of margins.

Bulldog's leaders devised a quick plan to move the Hatchet Force from the landing zone to the crash site to bring relief to recon team Flatfoot, and any of the helo crews that may have miraculously survived their crashes. As Hatchet Force Bulldog moved out, it became painfully clear they would be exposed far more than would be acceptable. There was very little cover to mask their movement. Seventy-five men ditty bopping right up to the crash site was a recipe for getting annihilated. Staring menacingly down on Bulldog's position was a ridge that ran roughly in the direction Bulldog needed to travel. Should the NVA already be behind the ridgeline, they would be holding the high ground, having cover and clear firing lanes to any movement below. Semi-automatic weapons like an AK-47, or worse yet, a machine gun, could have been humped up the hill and set up behind the ridge. Should R.P.Gs (rocket propelled grenades) be launched from this position, they would rip into Bulldog's flanks and place them in an even worse position than Flatfoot, the recon team they were supposed to rescue or recover.

U.S. Air Force Skymaster, the forward air controller (FAC) was SOG's link to the air assets that often kept them alive. Sketch by Star Barkman.

Lloyd Fisher quickly gathered a small group of Cambodians. They would provide flank security and explore what was behind the ridgeline. At the same time, Master Sergeant Minnicks and Sergeant First Class Robert Cavanaugh would investigate Bulldog's left flank which was down slope from Bulldog's main body. Minnicks and Cavanaugh would also take a small contingent of Cambodians with them. The decision to use flank security was a no brainer. It was directly out of Small Unit Tactics 101. Special Forces could do it in their sleep. Lieutenant Gamble Dick would take the main body of Bulldog in an easterly direction with the knowledge that his flanks were covered by Fisher and Minnicks, the two senior NCOs who were the "crème de la crème'" when it came to professionalism. The knee-high elephant grass that could grow to heights of 20 feet and reach a thickness that would retard a bullet's progress was sickly, thin, and provided Bulldog with no concealment. Hundreds of years of heavy rain had washed any topsoil to the bottom of the mountain. Despite the lack of friendly terrain, Bulldog's three elements began their approach to the crash site and Flatfoot's last known position.

Although the terrain proved to be totally uncooperative, Kip Kippenhan's 02—Cessna flew over Bulldog and gave the Hatchet Force some assurance that help was only a radio call away. Kippenhan had already informed the Army Gladiators of Bulldog's location. He also had the Air Force's A1-E Skyraiders on station. They too were informed of Bulldog's position and intentions. The Gladiators and A1-Es were the only place Bulldog could hang their hats right now. It was comforting to know they were already on station, briefed, and ready to strike. For a guy with a spastic colon, Kippenhan was really on his game. Both his flying and his voice provided Bulldog with much needed confidence.

Bulldog's main body moved steadily towards their objective but with great caution. They hoped to locate recon team Flatfoot and any survivors from the downed helicopters. The Hatchet Force had to restrain themselves. Walking into a trap was a very real possibility. It was unlikely the NVA had abandoned the mountainside after experiencing some success. The Hatchet Force continued to make slow progress when they were totally taken by surprise by an A1-E Skyraider that broke through the clouds and thundered across their path. It had been eerily silent until the Skyraiders scared the living shit out of all of them. Fortunately the pilot recognized Bulldog as a friendly, Major Jimmie Kilborne had been at the controls. Had an enemy element been caught in the open where Bulldog was they would have all been killed.

The A1-E Skyraider was an ideal aircraft to support troops on the ground. Capable of carrying a terrifying load of ordnance, the pilots often looked to get involved. Over 8,000 pounds of ordnance could be carried. Bombs, torpedoes, unguided rockets, or gun pods could make up the weight. In addition, 4 x 20 millimeter cannons made "Sandy" a lethal and long serving aircraft from 1945 to 1968. Over Hill 891 no fewer than 4 pilots received awards for their participation. Unbeknownst to the pilots, their beloved aircraft was soon to be retired again and this time for good.

Working above the main body of the Hatchet Force, Lloyd Fisher's security detail continued to maneuver itself to keep abreast with the larger group down slope from them.

It was essential to secure the ground lest an NVA machine gun team tear into the main body of Bulldog's flank.

Lieutenant Dick commanded Bulldog's main group. The progress they made towards the crash site was affected greatly by 2 elements: (1) the absolute need to use the utmost caution; and (2) the terrain that all 3 of Bulldog's elements encountered.

The main body's tempo quickly came to a halt. Each man took a knee and alternated looking outboard and keeping the muzzles of their weapons pointing out as well. There was complete silence. No shots had been fired and there were no NVA in sight. Hand signals were the only form of communication and Lloyd Fisher's "Bodes" had been schooled and were applying their lessons well. Word had reached Dick that Sergeant Minnicks and Sergeant Cavanaugh had discovered the wreckage of an Army Huey, presumably that of Warrant Officers Woolridge and Zanow. The Huey was a total wreck but there were no bodies to be found; however, a blood trail was soon found leading away from the wreckage. Sergeant First Class Robert Cavanaugh continued to follow the droplets and blood smears found on some low lying leaves and on the elephant grass. Using the muzzle of his rifle, the Sergeant parted a clump of elephant grass where he found a small pile of bloody bandages. Upon examination it was determined the bandages were clearly U.S. issue, so at least one crewman was injured and on the move. But the blood trail soon ran cold and both Minnicks and Cavanaugh back tracked to the wreckage. Standard operating procedure now dictated that the helo, what was left of it, be blown up so the NVA would be denied any use of its remains. Minnicks hustled his group out of the immediate area and Cavanaugh took care of the demolition work.

This part of the mission took on the characteristics of an investigation as opposed to a rescue or recovery. With each new discovery time was consumed not only for Minnicks group but for Bulldog in general. The primary objective of reaching the desperate recon team and the Jolly Green crash site was jeopardized by the consumption of time. The late start from Phu Bai now became a factor for Bulldog. The process of moving 75 men across the face of the mountain more quickly would not be possible or safe. One other issue also contributed to the task at hand and that was the steepness of the slope. Bulldog now had to battle the mountain more with each footstep they took towards the beleaguered recon team.

Meanwhile, Fisher's men had already discovered how the steep mountainside would affect their ability to secure the top. The trek to the top was an ass kicker, but it was absolutely essential to Bulldog's well-being. Fisher's efforts did not uncover any sign of NVA activity on either their ascent or at the crest of Hill 891. Still not satisfied, he continued to lead his detail over the crest and they began to descend the reverse slope of Hill 891. The men struggled to keep their footing but the reverse slope was even more treacherous than what was on the other side. Maintaining traction was all but impossible and the men began to slip and slide into rocks and depressions, twisting their ankles in directions they were not designed to go. Lloyd Fisher had good cause to scour the reverse slope. Should they pass it up and an NVA unit remained hidden, they could later reappear and inflict heavy casualties on Bulldog. Fisher was far too experienced to leave the reverse side to chance. His conscience, training, and common sense just wouldn't allow him to take the easy way out.

Satisfied that the enemy had not left an unwanted and lethal surprise, the flank security began to ascend the reverse slope. They used an occasional sprig of brush for a hand-hold and pushed the toes of their boots against any secure rocks to aid the climb back to the top. This was a much more difficult climb than the first and their upper legs burned. In addition, their lungs demanded more oxygen than was available. Fisher, now 37 years old, and his men were utterly exhausted. They were covered in sweat and dirt, not to mention pissed off. Fisher had survived many

That Empty Feeling

missions and close calls and remained alive by refusing to take the easy way out, or passing on short cuts.

Lieutenant Dick's primary force moved towards the direction of the Jolly Green crash site and where the recon team was. Their direction was determined through radio contact with Kipp Kippenhan flying above the crash site and Flatfoot. Continuing to move with caution, the column quickly came to a standstill when the leading riflemen shouldered their weapons and pointed the muzzles towards a shallow grassy draw to the front and left of the column. Startled, most every rifle was shouldered. Had they run into the NVA? The answer came quickly when a slim, blond-haired American strode nonchalantly out of the draw. His olive drab flight suit identified him as a Huey crewman. He identified himself as Specialist 4 Jarvis. He had been the door gunner on the UH-1D Huey, call sign Spartan 53. He walked back to Lieutenant Dick's position and did not appear to have any noticeable injury which was remarkable considering the pile of rubble that was once his helicopter. He was totally in control of his faculties and told the Lieutenant he was OK. "What about the rest of the crew?" He told Dick that both pilots, Kent Woolridge and Bill Zanow, had sustained injuries although he didn't know how severe they were. He did know they had both been rescued by a VNAF Kingbee helicopter earlier in the day. It was absolutely miraculous. That good news was tempered by his belief that Crew Chief Bill Whitney may have been killed, but he didn't know where he was. Dick radioed the Covey Fac for a helicopter to evacuate Specialist Jarvis. The helo showed up not long after and he was evacuated to safety without incident. Before leaving, Jarvis told Dick that the NVA had set up a heavy machine gun somewhere across from the base of the mountain. That information was greatly appreciated, and it reinforced the need to move with care.

Back with the 19th Assault Helicopter Company, Specialist Jarvis was debriefed by his commanding officer, Major David Hagler. The officer was astonished to find the gunner, "articulate in describing his ordeal in vivid detail." Forty years later Hagler recalls Jarvis' interview. "He told of helping the other crew members out of the aircraft and making them as comfortable as possible before climbing up the hill to seek help from the remaining members of the recon party. On the way up he became aware of the approach of a large helicopter . . . just as he came into the clearing he described seeing a fully uniformed North Vietnamese soldier come out of the tree line and boldly take up a firing position between him and the hovering helicopter that he recognized as a USAF "Jolly Green Giant." The enemy soldier facing away from Jarvis commenced firing an AK-47 toward the HH-3." He continued to explain, "moments later sparks began to come out of one of the engines . . ." At that point he described the helicopter as making a slow turn and roll over before the main rotor struck the ground and it began to break apart and burst into flames. He said "I could feel the heat and hear the screams from inside the Jolly Green as I helplessly stood there." Due to the flying debris and the NVA rifleman, Jarvis withdrew back down the hill toward the Spartan crash site. Suddenly he found himself on the receiving end of gunships that were "firing all over the place with rockets and machine guns." "I buried myself under a huge log to try to save myself from being killed by the heavy friendly fire." At first light he made his way down hill to his own crashed helicopter where he discovered that Bill Whitney had died during the night.

Short of being killed or captured, Jarvis had accrued nearly every negative experience a Huey crewman could possibly imagine. He had survived a horrifying crash, came nose to nose with an NVA rifleman, heard the sickening screams from Jolly 26, witnessed the mangled bodies of his fellow crewmen, and had been shot at by helicopters from his own company.

Jarvis had spoken with poise to Hatchet Force leader Gamble Dick and impressed his CO, Major David Hagler, while describing his ordeal. However, he later had contacted Russell Berger with some disturbing symptoms he hoped the medic could assist him with. Berger claimed to have treated Jarvis who complained about getting irregular sleep. He also confided that his hair color had taken on some ashen tones. He told the medic he had crashed while on a classified mission and was forced to hide from the N.V.A. Jarvis insisted his confession be kept strictly off the record. Berger agreed.

Bulldog's search and rescue mission had yielded some positive results. Jarvis had been rescued, the fate of Zanow and Woolridge had been learned, and the location of an NVA machine gun had been revealed. Not long after the helo picked up Jarvis, Lieutenant Dick's radio belched out a muffled "Bulldog Leader," it was Master Sergeant Minnicks' voice. He had discovered the lifeless body of Bill Whitney. There could be no joy in discovering the body; it was not an achievement. The only solace was that his family would have a body to mourn and lay to rest, or so they thought.

It was later learned that Bill Whitney had initially survived the crash and was found by pilot Kent Woolridge. Woolridge had been knocked unconscious and to this day has no idea how long he remained in that state. When he regained consciousness he began to stumble his way away from the wreck. He found Whitney in very bad condition. His breathing was labored and quickly went to shallow. His clothes were covered with blood, and he occasionally coughed up a pink frothy liquid which indicated he had damaged his lungs. Woolridge cradled Whitney's head in his only functioning arm. It was the only comfort he could give. The end came within minutes. The outstanding crew chief who could have easily avoided service had lost his personal battle on Hill 891 in Laos.

Whitney had failed his initial physical for military duty when he was found to have a hernia which he probably acquired while wrestling in high school. It was the perfect "out," a medical excuse endorsed by Uncle Sam. All he had to do was endure the hernia. Instead, he chose to have it surgically treated, and after a brief recuperation, he voluntarily subjected himself to a second physical and passed.

In his letters home to his brother Terry, Bill went to great lengths to minimize the considerable danger he actually faced. He recommended the Army Warrant Officer Program to all his brothers. He spoke highly of Woolridge and Zanow and was friends with them and Jarvis. He was proud to serve with his fellow crew members and by all accounts they were a smooth functioning team. Two of Whitney's commanding officers, Major David Hagler and Captain Ware, were present at the Marine mortuary to identify Whitney's body as called for by Army regulations. The procedure deeply touched Hagler who watched the Marine personnel prepare the body. "The gentle dignity that they exhibited in processing the remains of Bill Whitney was quite impressive." Hagler watched and was relieved and grateful they were "taking care to maintain a special respect for him as would be expected." Hagler also recalled them "removing the bracelet made from the links of a tail rotor pitch change chain that was a badge of honor among helicopter crew chiefs at the time."

However, all the good will the Marines worked for was quickly negated when Whitney's body failed to be sent home for thirty days. It caused an already grieving family more grief and denied them a timely closure.

It is likely the case that all wars create chaos and screw-ups are almost assured, yet Vietnam seemed to have more than its share. There was already a growing distrust of the military and the American government. As more and more American bodies came home, more and more Americans questioned why we are there. Men in the field were caught between their love of country and the rising anti-war sentiment. It was no wonder a segment of our returning warriors felt cheated and became disenchanted with the treatment they received from their fellow Americans and their own country.

As much as any family member, Bill's brother, Terry, was deeply affected by the loss of his brother, so much so that he named his son William. He later graduated from the Merchant Marine Academy and that made the loss of his uncle more bearable. A memorial service was held in honor of Bill in his home state of Utah. The service was complete with a missing man flyover. It was much appreciated by the family and helped ease their burden. It should be noted that services such as the one in Utah were not commonplace. For Americans killed in Vietnam memorials, statues and other tributes were also conspicuously absent.

Spartan 53 had taken a direct hit from a rocket propelled grenade. The blast knocked the stick out of the pilots' hands sending the helo to the ground. Woolridge's last memory was "chasing the stick around the cabin" in a last ditch effort to regain control. But it was too late and the UH-D with its crew of four crashed on Hill 891, rolled several times and broke into thousands of pieces, finally coming to a resting place in a slight depression.

Kent Woolridge had been knocked unconscious when his Huey collided with Hill 891. He was thrown clear of the wreckage and laid in the elephant grass for an unknown amount of time. A deep scalp laceration sent blood streaming down the side of his face. That was the least of his wounds. His upper left arm had been grotesquely shattered. The bones protruded through the skin and caused immense pain. The tissue and muscle surrounding the break had the consistency of raw stew meat. The wound had not been tended to and just begged for infection to set in. As if his injuries and witnessing Whitney's final breath weren't enough, the NVA began to probe the crash site and circled like jackals. Had Woolridge and Zanow been trained by the Air Force, they would have taken a comprehensive course on escape and evasion. The course was geared to pilots who found themselves behind enemy lines as a result of getting shot down or experiencing mechanical failure. It was taught in a serious fashion and taken in a serious manner. Unfortunately, the Army pilots did not receive serious instruction in this skill. Warrant Officer Woolridge would now have to rely on his own creativity and self-preservation skills.

The scalp laceration Woolridge received had left him tired and pale. While he lay unconscious, he must have looked very much like he was dead. He came to this conclusion while he was playing a serious game of hide and seek with the NVA. Hearing their voices, he reached for his Army issued .38 revolver which had been secured in his shoulder holster. He was shocked to learn it was missing. So too were his flight gloves. It was clear to him he had been robbed while unconscious and his .38 and gloves were now the trophies of a proud NVA soldier. Losing the .38 was not a big deal. It would have been a very poor choice of weapons considering the NVA were carrying AK-47 assault rifles.

On the other hand, the revolver might come in handy when the alternative was to fall into the hands of Uncle Ho's guys. The NVA had a very bad track record when it came to the treatment of prisoners. The most humane treatment you could expect would be to be shot where you were captured. The other alternative was to be paraded through the streets of Hanoi followed by an all expense paid trip to the fabulous Hanoi Hilton (prison). There you might receive a therapeutic back massage (beating with bamboo sticks), your shoulders dislocated or your teeth smashed out. If you were fed, your meal would be of the vilest contents, and malnutrition was guaranteed. One close look at Senator John McCain's broken body is proof positive that pilots and crew would do almost anything to avoid taking up residence in the Hilton.

It was a very long night for Warrant Officer Woolridge. He concealed himself in the brush for the dark hours, lying low and hoping daylight would bring rescue help. His arm had been caught between the seat and the door. The pain was unrelenting. When the J.G.s showed up Woolridge became a spectator; first watching the hair rising rescue piloted by Jack McTasney and then witnessing the crash and subsequent fire that consumed Jolly 26. He had heard the voices of the NVA and the screams from the crew of Jolly 26. When daylight arrived Woolridge found a piece of broken Plexiglas and used it to signal U.S. aircraft flying overhead. At least one A-1E spotted the signaling and reported it to Rescue Command. Somewhere along the long and very confused Air Force communication system, the signaling became insignificant. The pilots and crews from the 190th A.H.C. had all volunteered to stay and fly in support of SOG missions. Had Kent Woolridge, only twenty-two years old, known what he had gotten himself into?

Ho Chi Minh's educational curriculum was conspicuously missing the rules laid out for the treatment of prisoners as stated in the Geneva Convention. Kent Woolridge's luck held when he was spotted by a Vietnamese Air Force helicopter (VNAF) that swooped down to the crash site. Once on board the Kingbee, Woolridge was the recipient of a shot of morphine administered by an American medic. Warrant Officer Kent Woolridge was beginning the long journey home. He would receive a medical discharge in 1970, but not before being sent to Madigan Army Hospital in Tacoma, Washington. His recovery was not without a series of operations that included bone graphs, a metal plate and screws, and more bone graphs. His arm became shortened following the shoot down and he never regained full range of motion, thereby disqualifying him as an Army flight instructor. Refusing to accept that he would no longer be able to fly, Woolridge reinvented his career and began crop dusting, again at the controls of a helicopter. In 1975, he purchased a business and continues to this day piloting helicopters.

The "peter pilot" or copilot for Spartan 53 was William Zanow. In November of 1967 Zanow was 20 years old. He had been assigned to the 190th Assault Helicopter Company that was sent north to I Corp in support of Marine operations. When the Marines solved their own helicopter problems, Warrant Officer Zanow and crew received orders that dedicated them to SOG operations working out of FOB #1 at Phu Bai. He had never heard of SOG because it was classified but the kid from upstate New York quickly learned plenty about SOG operations. He quickly built an admiration for the 30 plus year old Special Forces sergeants that took their recon teams deep into Laos. On one occasion Zanow had been involved in inserting an experienced team, and only three days later he viewed their body bags lying next to a dusty runway. He was shocked but it wouldn't be the last time.

He was amazed at how a 20 year-old Warrant Officer could live an easier existence and make more than a 37 year old Master Sergeant. It was just baffling to him. On the night of November 8, 1967, William

Zanow's "easy" existence abruptly ended when he found himself dazed and bleeding on the side of Hill 891 in Laos. Spartan 53 had been shot down by an NVA soldier using a rocket propelled grenade fired from only 150 feet away. The grenade crashed into the rotor system, and in less than 3 seconds, the Huey crashed and rolled down the mountainside throwing the four man crew helter skelter to the ground. Semi-conscious, Zanow was unable to move without great pain. He also discovered he had left all of his front teeth on the instrument panel. Broken off at the gum line he had only ragged and sharp stubs remaining. He did a cursory search for the $15 grease gun he had purchased. The gun was a relic used by World War II tankers. It was light weight, easy to store, very noisy and totally inaccurate. Still it was an upgrade from his .38 which he surrendered to Specialist Jarvis when they found one another in some low lying brush. Completely out of gas, Zanow instructed Jarvis to climb to the top of the hill and get help, not knowing there was no help to be had.

Zanow had taken the Army escape and evasion class which consisted of only 16 hours of instruction and practical application. The instruction had been very rinky-dink and besides, he had no energy or strength to do anything but hide and hope Jarvis returned. It was a very long night. Zanow witnessed 2 helos shot down and heard the NVA prowling the crash site. However, the most terrifying event was the strafing by the Army Gladiators with their mini-guns blazing. They had no idea who was alive or dead but the NVA seemed to be kept at bay by the attack helos. In the morning a VNAF helo passed overhead and he waved his white T shirt at them. They took a second pass, swooped in and pulled him on board. He was flown to Phu Bai Hospital where the Vietnamese pilot made a rather hard landing, scaring everyone aboard except the pilot. After a 2 week stay and having been presented with the Purple Heart (very informally), Zanow walked out without authorization, and wearing a borrowed set of Marine utilities, hitch-hiked back to the 190th Assault Helicopter Company. He finished his first tour of duty in Vietnam, served in Germany and returned to Southeast Asia for a second tour. He was shot down a second time at just over 21 years of age. He finally accepted the fact that he was mortal. On his second tour, while instructing South Vietnamese pilots, he discovered one of his students turned out to be the very same pilot that rescued him from Hill 891.

When the flank security lead by Sergeant Fisher and Sergeant Minnicks detail rejoined Bulldog's main force the mission to clean up the mess continued. The primary goal of finding recon team Flatfoot and locating Jolly Green 26 resumed, however, time had been consumed and although necessary, dividing the Hatchet Force brought an unsettling affect on everyone. Fisher and Minnicks' return was a psychological lift, especially for Lieutenants Hoepner and Dick.

Throughout Bulldog's journey from the L.Z. they caught glimpses of Marine attack helos prowling on the periphery of Hill 891. There was some comfort in that. The Marines had pioneered close air support with fixed wing aircraft prior to World War II. Their helo pilots had carried air support doctrine a step further now with Huey helicopters. Their pilots had collected some impressive credentials while in Southeast Asia.

Gamble Dick's radio crackled with a voice not yet heard from. It was a U.S.M.C. gunship pilot operating in support of Bulldog's mission. The pilot reported seeing an American exiting a wood line approximately a thousand meters from Bulldog's position. The Huey attack ship was under-powered, like all Hueys, and had reported being nearly bingo on fuel. The pilot (name unknown) felt he could effectively land and take on the badly burned pilot but was unsure his aircraft could then take off. The equation was further complicated by what aviation referred to as D.A.F., or density altitude factor. It made taking off in heat, humidity and high altitude a struggle. Despite the circumstances, the Marine pilot was aware that the Air Force, Army, and South Vietnamese pilots had all landed and then taken off successfully.

In the end, the aircraft commander could not allow a fellow countryman to fall into the hands of the ruthless N.V.A. Also looking timid or less than aggressive was not in a Marine's DNA and the pilot quickly sent his ship towards earth. The Marine gunner quickly pulled the battered and burned pilot aboard and the takeoff was now in the hands and feet of the pilot. The aircraft groaned under the load and seemed to take an eternity to gain altitude. Finally the pilot coaxed the Huey skyward and they were soon headed back to beautiful Khe Sanh.

Again Lieutenant Dick's radio came to life "Bulldog, Bulldog, this is Marine gun ship, we have American pilot on board. He is alive and was the aircraft commander for Jolly Green 26." The Marine air crew had rescued Air Force Captain Gerald O. Young. It was positive news for Bulldog who now could search for other survivors. At this point in time no one knew what Captain Young's physical status was or the incredible story of his actions and survival.

With the Marine gunship now heading back to Khe Sanh there were fewer aircraft available to assist Bulldog. No matter, the Hatchet Force pushed forward until they came to an area with dense vegetation that lay adjacent to a tree line. Jolly Green 26 had reportedly rolled into a ravine. Did this vegetation cover that ravine? Bulldog's lead element waded into the underbrush and quickly found the mouth of a crevasse at the top.

The point man was a Cambodian mercenary who mistakenly led the entire patrol into the crevasse. Although the Bode moved ahead with caution it was not what Lieutenant Dick felt a prudent move. Before the Lieutenant could make his way to the front of the column to steer his group around the crevasse, the entire element had been swallowed by the depression and continued to move further into the stomach and then into the bowels of an all-consuming monster. It had a grave-like feel to it that went unacknowledged. There was no mistaking the musty fetid smell that failed to evacuate the nostrils. The walls of the depression grew higher with each passing step, and in some places reached 20 feet high. In some spots the crevasse was only 3 feet wide and it became apparent a helicopter could not roll into the narrow opening.

The Cambodians were also known as the "KKK," which stood for Khymer Kompuchea Krom, which basically stated they were from the Mekong Delta region. Identifying themselves in this way separated them from other tribes and from native Vietnamese. Cambodian groups were not fond of each other, and those living within Vietnam's borders often met with racism. The "Bodes" had no second thoughts about soldering against the Vietnamese. As mercenaries, the KKK earned the respect of America's Special Forces, men many of whom considered them as allies and comrades.

However, as skilled as the KKK became in the field, they could at times become rather superstitious. The deep crevasse began to unnerve the troops and they could be seen clutching their amulets. An amulet was a little bag of rice that had been blessed by Buddhist Priests and was roughly equivalent to the Catholic Rosary. The leader of the mercenary force was Ah Soc Chan. It didn't take him long before he caught wind of the serious effect the subterranean reconnaissance was having on his men.

Mr. Chan was no ordinary mercenary. He was highly educated and fluent in English, French, Vietnamese and Khymer. The Special Forces soldiers referred to Ah Soc Chan as "Sam." Brevity was the motive for the Americanization of his given name. Despite Sam's effective leadership and communication skills there were some Americans who felt he was made privy to plans and information that should not have been divulged to non-Americans. Later Sam left FOB#1 because of his wife's illness; he did not return.

Sam soon approached the Lieutenant blurting out that "The soldiers are very scared, this is not a good place to be, and we must leave this place." Dick responded "Tell the men we are looking for a way out." Sam disappeared to the rear of the column to deliver the good news to his men.

The Green Beret Lieutenant looked up at the walls on each side and knew how easily just one NVA soldier armed with grenades or an AK-47 could wipe them out in short order. Bulldog moved 50 more meters and an opening appeared leading east. The main body needed to go west to meet their other groups left behind. Despite the wrong direction Dick decided to take the opening. Anywhere seemed a good choice compared to where they were. There was one small problem with following the opening; the return trip would be straight up hill. The slope was steep and sweat seeped through their shirts as the workload increased. Some grunting could be heard but there were no complaints. Everyone was relieved to escape the claustrophobia the ravine brought on them.

Once again, time had been exchanged for thoroughness and with the entire force now together they forged ahead toward the trapped recon team. Covering less than 100 meters, Dick's radio came alive with the voice of the Covey Fac. A beeper signal had been picked up 600 meters from where Captain Young had been rescued that would have made it over a thousand meters from Bulldog's position. The Air Force wanted it checked out. Dick laid his compass on top of the map and determined his Hatchet Force was travelling away from the beeper and were heading towards the Jolly Green crash site. The Air Force was concerned another crewman was using the beeper. They were totally clueless about the terrain and the difficulty the slope had on moving 75 men around. Bulldog could not run from pillar to post checking out every new piece of intelligence that came in. Besides, this mission was closing in on the 10 hours allotted, exfiltration time was soon approaching.

With both the Army and now the Air Force tugging at Bulldog's collar, Gamble Dick took several minutes and then radioed the Cessna (forward air controller), "Covey this is Bulldog, do you read?" "Bulldog, this is Covey, go." Dick continued "Be advised we cannot reach your beeper site or the crash site before dark. We are going to find a pick up zone so the choppers can get us out for the night, over. Covey came back." "Bulldog be advised that severe weather will keep helos grounded, advise you seek RON (remain overnight area)." Lieutenant Hoepner was eaves-dropping on the radio conversation and just caught the letters RON. He said nothing but the "What the fuck is going on?" look was hard to miss.

Hadn't Major Snell said everyone was to be out before dark? Wasn't this supposed to be a 10 hour mission? Hatchet Force Bulldog was not totally prepared to stay the night. Few had packed the extra dry clothing necessary, ponchos were left back at Phu Bai. Poncho liners for cold mountain nights had been left at the Phu Bai landing zone, c-rations had not been drawn, and water was already in short supply. Only a few Claymore mines had been packed in for night defensive purposes, and E tools (entrenching shovels) had been left in the rear. The experienced N.C.O.s and officers knew they could not allow the men to sense their frustration or anger. The best had to be made of a very dangerous situation. There was nothing to do now but hump to the top of Hill 891 and prepare the best night defensive position possible.

Bulldog began the arduous task of moving up the steep slope. After moving about 150 meters, a dull sounding thump was heard near the rear of the Hatchet Force. Word was quickly passed up that there was a casualty that needed immediate treatment. Ron Bock, whose specialty was treating combat wounds in the field, hustled to the fallen victim and arrived before the smoke and dust had settled. The casualty was Special Forces Sergeant Erskine Osborne (Ozzy). He had stepped on a "toe popper" and quite possibly lay where other poppers were left. Ron Bock directed the men to move Ozzy to a safe place and he began to treat the Sergeant for his wounds. The mine was made of plastic, stood only 3 inches tall, and was nearly undetectable in elephant grass or on the jungle floor. It was designed to maim and was an American weapon carried by the recon teams and left in their wake to slow down NVA pursuers. It was clear recon team Flatfoot had passed through this area and had left the device to slow down the NVA who were on their trail. The insidious little device was very effective at causing pain and suffering, but it could not distinguish the bad guys from the good and in its own peculiar way became what is known as "friendly fire."

Ozzy had intentionally moved into a treed area for the purpose of scouting that area. Osborne found no sign of the NVA but did have the misfortune to discover an American anti-personnel mine. Ron Bock recalled the event, "Master Sergeant Charles Harper and I went to aid Ozzy and carried him out." Like several others, Charles Harper had jumped in to lend a hand to the Hatchet Force. Harper's only motivation was his friendship with Master Sergeant Bruce Baxter who was reportedly in serious trouble on Hill 891. Lacking a towering presence, Harper brought strength and experience to Bulldog's considerable force.

Once to a safer area Bock began to treat Ozzy's wound. "The mine had blown off about half of the front foot. The rubber from the sole of his jungle boot was blown up into his foot and prevented it from bleeding. He was in much pain and I gave him a morphine shot. I placed an Army issue tourniquet loosely on his ankle to be tightened if needed. Otherwise it was best to leave it as it was so that circulation would continue to the injured part of the foot. He was evacuated via helicopter with an indigenous soldier who was suffering from stomach pains."

Bock recollected that SFC Osborne "was the senior engineer on our team from the 1st Special Forces Group. He was a career soldier, served in the 10th Special Forces Group prior to coming to the 1st and had a Combat Infantry Badge from prior service in Vietnam. He had recently graduated from the 1st Special Forces Scuba School, as had SFC Brooke Bell and SFC Gilbert Hamilton, who were all on the mission to Hill 891." A native West Virginian, Osborne was described as a "very professional soldier."

Gamble Dick radioed for a medevac that showed up within 30 minutes and successfully whisked Sergeant First Class Osborne to Phu Bai Hospital. Between Bock's field medicine and the professional work at Phu Bai, Osborne was able to keep the part of his foot that was left and avoid an amputation. Recovery would not be easy and the affects would last forever.

In addition to Osborne, Ron Bock had also treated one of the Cambodians who had complained of stomach problems. Bock felt the mercenary had eaten reconstituted rice and had failed to soak in water for the prescribed amount of time. The rice had allied itself with the always present nervous condition that stalked men who soldiered in dangerous places. Bent over and cramping, the Cambodian was also placed on the outbound chopper. He created a small stir while being loaded as he did not want to go alone. Another Cambodian quickly jumped on the Huey to escort his buddy to the South Vietnamese hospital. Cambodians often met with prejudicial treatment from the South Vietnamese who viewed them as inferior. A body guard was deemed a necessary precaution. There was fear that the treatment would be more dangerous than the affliction.

Bulldog regrouped and began to make its way to the top of Hill 891. The men found the climb to be taxing and it resulted in a shortage of oxygen in their lungs. They continued along the ridgeline until Master Sergeant Fisher and Minnicks concurred they had found a spot suitable for their overnight stay. As light was beginning to diminish, the men began to improve their position for defending against an NVA attack should one materialize.

Sergeant First Class Robert Cavanaugh, like the rest of the Special Forces men on the mission, failed to bring an E-tool to Hill 891. After all, a 10 hour "look see" mission would not require the entrenching tool since it would only slow him down. One thing the Sergeant did not leave back in Phu Bai was a fancy survival vest loaded with pockets and compartments. It had been a gift from a grateful downed pilot rescued by a Recon team Cavanaugh was a member of. None of the compartments could hold an E-tool, but the Special Forces man always packed in an ample supply of his favorite survival food, Slim Jims. The rolled beef would not help dig a fighting hole but would come in handy at dinner time. For the time being the Sergeant would have to rely on his survival knife to gouge out a protective depression in the boney soil.

As the RON (remain overnight position) was being worked on, Lieutenant Dick received a message from one of the Huey gunships. They advised Bulldog that they were Bingo on fuel and had to leave the area of operations. Dick requested the gunship expend all remaining ordnance where crash survivor Jarvis had pointed out an NVA machine gun was set up. The Huey looped around lining up its attack run and unleashed a torrent of machine gun fire and 3.5 millimeter rockets on the suspected target. There was no return fire, but the Huey crew was right on target.

Bob Cavanaugh at the Larry W. Maysey statue in Chester, NJ, 2010. SFC Cavanaugh found Maysey's body on Hill 891 and was nearly killed himself hours later. Photo courtesy of Terry Arentowicz.

Gamble Dick's sketch shows Huey attack helos working hillside while U.S.A.F. forward air controller controls the scene.

The remaining gunship came up on Dick's radio also. They requested Bulldog mark their position for future reference. Sergeant Cavanaugh grabbed the strobe light, fully extended his 6'3" frame and turned on the strobe light as requested. A nervous gunner mistook the strobe for ground fire intended to knock the Huey out of the sky. The door gunner opened up with his M-60 sending a stream of bullets right over Cavanaugh's head nearly killing him. An unfortunate Cambodian sitting near Cavanaugh was sprayed with bullet fragments and chipped rock.

Ron Bock saw the entire mishap take shape. In the fading light he actually saw the gunner prepping his gun but the entire event went so fast he could do nothing to stop it. Once again the Texas-born Bock was called upon to treat one of the Cambodians. Although the mercenary was hit, his wounds were not life threatening. It was a good thing because there would be no medevac at this hour. Ron Bock managed to keep the Bode comfortable throughout the night.

Bulldog's position was now engulfed in total darkness. Night time always brought out negative thoughts but this night seemed unusually dark and foreboding. At one end of Bulldog's perimeter Lieutenant Gamble Dick stood silently. He was joined by Master Sergeant Fisher, who in his usual understated way said, "Sir, this is really bad." Dick replied by saying, "I'd be surprised if we ever see another sunrise." Fisher's head moved slightly in the up and down direction.

The discussion had ended as fast as it started and the 2 men returned to supervising the fine tuning of their position, as untenable as it was. Fisher parted by quietly telling his Lieutenant, "We will be prepared and make a stand here, we may die. Then it will be somebody else's turn to come for us."

CHAPTER 10

LET THERE BE LIGHT

Hill 891, Laos, 2000 hours, 9 November, 1967

Bulldog found itself in a very precarious situation. They had entered Laos with a minimal amount of information and intelligence and now found themselves less prepared than they could have been. The Hatchet Force would have to assume a defensive posture without some of the essential tools employed by SOG teams at night.

Rick Bayer had packed in a few Claymore mines, which would be helpful but certainly not the number they were accustomed to. Two M-60 machine guns had been carried in by the Special Forces weapons experts. The guns were a huge hurdle for any enemy to clear but more would have been better. One low tech item was in short supply, entrenching tools (folding shovels). Without the means to dig in properly the team would be vulnerable to mortar attacks, machine gun fire, and rifle-propelled grenades. Although the team's position on the crown of the hill was a plus, they were compromised to both north and south by lesser slopes that had some cover on them in the form of trees and brush. That cover could provide the NVA with good avenues to approach Bulldog's night position and possibly negate the effectiveness of the machine guns which would cover the most likely areas the NVA would launch attacks from.

To the north lay the near vertical slope Master Sergeant Fisher's group had probed earlier in the day. An approach from the north would be the most physically challenging for the NVA. However, the NVA had established a history of using challenging terrain, and it was on the northern edge of Bulldog's perimeter that Lloyd Fisher and Lieutenant Dick selected to establish their command post. It was here the all important PRC-25 (radio) would be operated and defended by Fisher and Dick. It was vital the radio remain secure. To Bulldog's south lay the area where Flatfoot (recon team) was thought to be and where the helicopter attempted to land and rescue Flatfoot. Looking at the terrain, Dick wondered how any helicopter could attempt a rescue on the steep slope without their rotors striking the mountainside, and at night no less. It had been an amazing bit of airmanship. Somewhere in that general vicinity was Jolly Green 26 and its crew along with Bruce Baxter, Joseph Kussick and maybe even others, provided they made it through the night. Bulldog would probe that area. They may meet the NVA in a stand of brush, or they may meet them from a tree line. If it took a fight to clean up the mess, so be it. There was no other option. Bulldog would get their opportunity either to rescue or recover their fellow Americans, but first they must make it through the night.

The Truong Song Mountains grew cold and uncomfortable at night. Lloyd Fisher and Gamble Dick had only one poncho liner between them. The other had been used to wrap "Ozzy" in so he wouldn't go into shock. Poncho liners were quilted lightly and rectangular in shape. They were designed to go under the rubberized poncho. The liners were as close to cold weather gear as could be found in Southeast Asia. The two Special Forces men huddled inside the poncho liner. It was a small gesture between two different men. One was an officer with less experience and more education, and the other a non-commissioned officer with less education and a ton of experience. They did have the cold, hunger and the fear of the unknown in common. Getting comfortable was absolutely out of the question, but the rock pressing against the Lieutenant's leg had to go. The rock turned out to be the can of peaches he had stashed in his cargo pocket just before leaving Phu Bai. What a find! A quick search of his pockets turned up the tiny hinged can opener (known as a P-38) that came with C-rations. A brown plastic spoon came from the same breast pocket. Fisher sat silently and soon the sweet smell of ripe peaches wafted to him shortly followed by the can being pressed into his hand. Dick had left some peaches and the thick syrup was every bit as tasty and sugary as the fruit itself. Sharing this delicacy was much more than just a kind gesture; it was the ultimate act of camaraderie.

The peaches were consumed quickly but the night would not end and sleep might lead to the demise of the entire team. Tree branches began to look like AK-47s. Every shadow took the shape of an NVA helmet and the nocturnal animals seemed to speak some sort of Vietnamese dialect. The night played some very serious tricks with the mind.

After all, Bulldog had not encountered a single NVA soldier and their only injuries had been inflicted by an American mine and a single case of dysentery brought on by poorly prepared rice. With any luck the NVA had withdrawn, satisfied by their shoot downs and killing of an unknown number of U.S. service personnel. Maybe they had suffered enough of their own casualties inflicted by the Huey attack ships and the Skyraiders.

At approximately 1230 hours members of the Hatchet Force began to hear the low growl of engines in the distance. The engine noise overhead belonged to a United States Air Force C-130 Hercules call sign "Blind Bat 03," quite possibly the most versatile aircraft in the Air Force's inventory. On the night of November 9, 1967, it was in the role of a flare ship. The aircraft had been launched from Udorn Royal Tai Air Base, Thailand, and came under the control of the 8th Tactical Fighter Wing.

As the engine volume built, Lieutenant Dick's PRC-25 belched "Bulldog, Bulldog this is Blind Bat 03, do you read?" In the dark Dick searched for the radio handset and then responded "Blind Bat 03 this is Bulldog, over." "Bulldog, Bat 3 is inbound to your location to turn on the lights, over." "Uh, say again your intentions Bat 3, over." "Bulldog, Bat 03 is a flare ship; just say the word and we will turn your night into day." C-130 crews were used to receiving positive responses from Special Forces teams on the ground. Richard A. Young, a crewman, had flown Blind Bat missions many times and recalled one Recon Team leader yelling in his microphone; "Let there be light and there was light; I can read a fucking newspaper down here!"

Fisher had been eavesdropping on Dick's radio conversation and moved his head up and down in approval of the flares. Both agreed that light might just be the pick-me-up the team needed and they quickly gave Bat 3 the go ahead to drop the flares. Attached to mini-parachutes, the magnesium-fueled flares swung gently back and forth and drifted lazily to the ground. The light created has often been described as eerie and ghostlike. The continued movement of the flares also made the trees, rocks, and shrubs appear to also be in motion.

U.S.A.F. C-130 Hercules served as a flare ship over Hill 891. It took on many jobs over Southeast Asia. Sketch by Star Barkman.

The light was artificial and surreal, but the overall effect was very positive and kept superior forces from forming up close to Bulldog's position. Blind Bat had denied the NVA the cover of darkness, but more importantly Bat 3's radio operator sent a positive stream of chatter to both Lloyd Fisher and Gamble Dick. Whether the radio man knew it or not, he was practicing psychology at 5,000 feet by injecting Bulldog's leaders with spirit lifting conversation, keeping them alert and providing some comedy as well.

At one point the radio man asked Dick if Bulldog was a large force or small. It had always been suspected that the NVA had electronic listening in capabilities. Dick responded that indeed Bulldog was a robust force so as not to allow the NVA to think they could overrun the Hatchet Force. Bat 3 responded, "That's good because it looks like a Boy Scout jamboree down there; you guys are completely surrounded by NVA campfires."

The "jamboree" information was sobering news and tossed a wet blanket on the theory the NVA had withdrawn. The NVA did not make things easy for SOG in Laos. They always seemed to be dogged in their pursuit to eliminate recon teams and cripple Hatchet Forces. Dick was so impressed with the jamboree information he requested Bat 3 get word to his girlfriend (now his wife) and parents that his last thoughts were of them. Bat 3 promised to deliver the information, but only if necessary.

The night was just getting started when the men began to catch flickers of lights off to the (east-southeast.) It was no coincidence that portions of the Ho Chi Minh Trail lay exactly in that direction. Like a never-ending snake, the light flickers methodically wound their way through the jungle below. It became apparent that the Hatchet Force was watching a mammoth NVA truck convoy heading south. The Chinese had leased thousands of large military type trucks. Master Sergeant Fisher quickly computed some grid coordinates and relayed them to Blind Bat 03. The C-130 in turn radioed Udorn Royal Tai Air Force Base in Thailand. The United States Air Force scrambled a flight of A1-E Skyraiders and Bulldog heard their radio chatter with Blind Bat 03. Both the Navy and Air Force had removed the A1-Es from moth balls and they had enjoyed great success. Like all aircraft the life span of the Skyraiders would finally come to an end before the war in Vietnam concluded. On this night the A1-Es could find no targets and returned to U-Dorn with a full load of unexpended ordnance. Although the convoy could be seen from the ground, the pilots could not locate it from the air. The Ho Chi

Minh Trail had plenty of natural camouflage, and where it was absent Ho's "trail keepers" built bamboo frames and attached vegetation to it to protect the trucks from the airborne hunters. The A1-E pilots could claim plenty of kills along the trail, but on this night the hunters could not locate their quarry. How many tons of war making materiel had been transported that night alone and why was this truck convoy so massive? These were questions William Colby's guys were supposed to answer with the help of SOG. The convoy would not go unreported. It should be kept in mind that the TET New Year attacks were not in the too distant future.

Lloyd Fisher felt the need for flares had diminished and requested Bat 3 hold the light show and conserve whatever flares they had left in case an attack was initiated by the NVA. Bat 3 concurred and informed Fisher they were leaving the immediate area for a short time. A half hour passed, and true to their word Bat 03 returned with news. They believed they had seen anti-aircraft guns being towed towards Bulldog's position. Should anti-aircraft guns make it to Bulldog's general area they would threaten Bulldog's ability to be exfiltrated by helicopter. It would create even more hazardous flying for the A1-Es and all other aircraft. Fisher sarcastically asked Blind Bat when the good news might be coming. Blind Bat responded that the good news was inbound in the form of their replacement. Blind Bat had to return to base as they were nearly bingo on fuel. "Lamplighter" was the call sign for Bat 3's replacement. They had been briefed and would be on station in just a few minutes. The few minutes passed and Lamplighter radioed they wanted to "kick out" a flare for ground adjustment. It was standard operating procedure and Bulldog approved. Minutes passed, and not only did Bulldog fail to see a flare but they could not even hear the powerful C-130 engines. During the next 20 minutes Lamplighter repeated the procedure without results. Lamplighter's radio man seemed to be agitated by the repeated failures, and when Bulldog asked if Lamplighter could see a ring of campfires a loud "negative" blurted back on Bulldog's radio. Finally, Lamplighter's pilot widened his orbit and Bulldog reported they could hear the C-130's engines. Lloyd Fisher immediately requested that all flares be held unless Lamplighter saw an exchange of green and orange tracers, and only then should the flares be dropped.

The comforting and even amusing rapport that Blind Bat had brought was now gone. Maybe Lamplighter wanted to get back to the

"O" Club, or maybe their crew preferred hunter killer missions along the trail. Those missions allowed the C-130 pilots to shoot at anything that moved; sometimes awards were bestowed. It was far more glamorous than kicking out flares into the dark of night and holding the hand of some SOG team you would never hear from again.

Lamplighter (C-130 flare ship) did assist with a request from Iron Spud, a Mohawk Army surveillance aircraft from the 131st Aviation Company. Iron Spud requested Lamplighter provide them with Bulldog's current situation. This request was dutifully complied with. Iron Spud assured Bulldog that the Army was aware of their current situation and would not forget them. SOG had worked with the Mohawk surveillance aircraft before and that work had been performed under dire conditions. A prearranged communication system had been worked out between the SOG units and the surveillance aircraft. It was simple; if the enemy was up close and personal with the hatchet force or recon team they would simply key the radio microphone once for an affirmative and twice for a negative answer. Hopefully Bulldog would not need to contact Iron Spud but it was a comfort the Army had contacted them.

Hill 891, Laos, 0630 hours, 10 November, 1967

With dawn breaking the American members of Bulldog began to check their perimeter. Every member was brought to full alert and weapons and ammo were made ready. This was preferred time for the NVA to mount an attack since the defenders would be exhausted both physically and psychologically from battling the dark hours. The minutes ticked by and slowly a few rays of daylight could be seen.

There had been no attacks, not even a probe, nothing at all. It was Murphy's Law in reverse. Had the screw turned in Bulldog's favor? On this morning the Hatchet Force need not wait for helicopters, they were already on the job. Today the mission would focus on finding Jolly Green 26's crew (status unknown) and processing the crash site. In addition, Joseph Kussick and Bruce Baxter would be located and hopefully rescued or at worst recovered, if need be. The mission would then be over and Bulldog would get exfiltrated by whoever had available helos and then flown to Phu Bai and safety. It was hard to think of Phu Bai as even a home away from home. As Sergeant First Class Robert Cavanaugh said, "I always felt safe in South Vietnam, safe compared to Laos that is."

Undoubtedly the mess sergeant would have the traditional steak and eggs for returning recon teams and Hatchet Forces. Kind of a Thanksgiving meal, a thanks for completing a mission alive.

CHAPTER 11

70 Pounds of Molten Metal

Like every other day in Southeast Asia the sky began to lighten, although on this day darkness seemed to loiter and be reluctant to leave. The fiery sun that usually brought stifling heat and oppressive humidity failed to fully appear. In the sun's absence a solid wall of leaden colored clouds bulldozed its way toward Hill 891. There was a mean look to the clouds. They were going to "piss" all over the mountainside.

Bulldog's plan would need revision. Unless the weather broke, the helos would not fly and breakfast would also have to be aborted due to a lack of food. Judging by the look in the sky, water, now in short supply, was on its way in. Hopefully they could get exfiltrated later in the day.

Hill 891, Laos, 0700 hours, 10 November, 1967

The plan for the day was simplified and called for Lieutenant Rod Hoepner to lead one group down the mountainside to search for the wreckage and hopefully the survivors of the Jolly Green 26 crash. Lieutenant Dick would remain with another group at the top of the hill and be prepared to reinforce Hoepner's search and rescue team should they come under attack. The last man in Lieutenant Hoepner's patrol had barely disappeared from view when a steady light rain replaced the misty drizzle that preceded it. The rain presented a double edged sword; it provided drinking water, relief from the heat, and it softened the earth so fox holes could be gouged out for better protection. However, should the rain increase in intensity it would fill the holes keeping the men wet and perhaps force them to remain overnight once again enduring the misery that it would bring. The only condition that could make for more misery would be an NVA attack. Why hadn't the NVA pursued Bulldog?

It has been over 40 years since SOG sent their recon teams and Hatchet Forces behind enemy lines and missions have yet to be forgotten. Gamble Dick offered some opinions as to where the NVA was and why they hadn't yet attacked.

First, he felt that SOG's decision to insert a larger number of men (75) than normally would be used caught the NVA with smaller units operating near Hill 891. The mountainous terrain and the weather slowed everyone down and time prevented them from building up a substantial force. Bulldog had been inserted by helo, but the NVA had no air capabilities and had to walk to where trucks couldn't travel.

The CIA was supposed to take the intelligence SOG turned over to them and make sense of it. However, throughout November of 1967 the NVA was in the process of moving the 325C, 304 and the 320th Divisions through Laos utilizing the Ho Chi Minh Trail. The CIA failed to connect the dots and the NVA did not want to bring any more unwanted attention to their increased use of the trail. Reports of divisions moving south may have been a wakeup call and tip the NVA's future plans to Colby's guys.

Both Flatfoot and Bulldog had landed and entered Laos near route B-45 (NVA route designation). It was an east-west spur that ran perpendicular to the Ho Chi Minh Trail. B-45 supplied NVA operations near the upper A Shau Valley which included Marine strongholds at Khe Sanh and Con-Thien. Should the NVA feel threatened in this area, it was possible they would pursue a recon team with more violence than normal. Had the NVA been eavesdropping on Bulldog's radio conversations, they would have realized Bulldog was on a rescue and recovery mission and decided on a less aggressive posture? Moving men and materiel was the NVA's short term goal. The grand prize was going to be the TET offensive of 1968 and what a prize it turned out to be.

Watching and waiting was an NVA virtue. Should Bulldog make any proactive moves there would be time to pounce on them as they had on Flatfoot.

Jolly Green 26 Crash Site, Hill 891, 1000 hours, 10 November, 1967

Late in the day on November 9, Covey 57 had spotted what the pilot described as 70 pounds of molten metal and fractured Plexiglas. He believed it to be part of the wreckage of Air Force Rescue Helicopter Jolly Green 26. Lieutenant Rod Hoepner had been briefed about the wreckage in hopes it would save his patrol time in locating it and conserve energy, both of which the men had in limited amounts.

Using the Covey report as a guide, Hoepner steered his patrol down hill. The drizzle and mist had loosened what little topsoil existed, making the descent as strenuous as an uphill climb. One Special Forces sergeant said it was ". . . slicker than cat shit on a linoleum floor." Traversing the side of the mountain as much as possible, Hoepner's men seemed to take turns losing their footing and then peeling themselves from the gooey mess. The walking and falling repeated until the men grew frustrated and an occasional curse word could be heard following a tumble. Already filthy, their trousers became caked with mud and their boots seemed to gain weight with each step.

Special Forces Sergeant Bruce Lutrell was the first to report finding a sizeable piece of wreckage. It appeared to be the flight deck from Jolly Green 26. Lutrell worked to untangle some of the twisted metal, and in so doing he discovered two bodies. Both bodies were wearing flight suits making them part of the Air Force Jolly Green 26 crew. Helicopter crews wore dog tags and Sergeant Lutrell indentified the remains as being Captain Ralph Brower, co-pilot from Jolly Green 26, and Sergeant Eugene Clay, 26's flight engineer. The unenviable task of untangling the 2 victims from what once was a helicopter fell to Sergeant First Class Bruce Lutrell and Bulldog's primary medic, Ron Bock. The mission to Hill 891 had already been an eventful one for Bock who was on his first tour and was making a big impression on his more experienced Special Forces team members.

The two victims, Eugene Clay and Ralph Brower, had flown to Hill 891 to rescue recon team Flatfoot. They now had to be recovered and returned to their families. The jagged and twisted aluminum clung stubbornly to the remains of the two aviators. Lutrell and Bock persevered working on the steep slope with the threat of being attacked always on their minds. Lieutenant Hoepner had provided some security around the wreckage by setting up a hasty perimeter. After a short time Lutrell and

Bock prevailed and liberated the remains of both Clay and Brower. They placed the two men together on a poncho, their dog tags still hanging from their necks. The war in Southeast Asia had ended for Brower and Clay. Their families would now be burdened by their loss, and the remains would be etched in the minds of Lutrell and Bock, never to leave.

Lieutenant Rod Hoepner's men continued to remain exposed to an NVA attack on the mountainside. In order to shorten their exposure time he had his men fan out to bring the recovery to a speedy and safe end. The job of recovery was not a rewarding one, and the gloomy weather contributed a depressing feeling to the men, although they never waivered and seemed resolute to finish the task at hand.

The team continued to scour the mountainside and soon Sergeant First Class Brooke Bell discovered the main cabin from the wrecked helicopter. Another body was found tangled in the wreckage. Bell began to extricate the body and was soon joined by Ron Bock. Together they were able to free the body and handled the remains with as much respect as could be given considering the circumstances. Bock checked for dog tags but found none, however, Bell was able to locate a section of metal that resembled a piece of tape measure. Both men immediately identified the object as an antenna from a PRC-25 radio. Extra long antennae were carried by SOG radio men to transmit and receive from longer distances. In addition to the antennae, radio parts were found in the wreckage and near the body.

Since SOG team members did not wear dog tags inside of neutral Laos and the body was devoid of tags, it was determined not to be an Air Force crew man. The radio parts lead Lutrell and Bock to conclude they had discovered the body of Specialist 4 Joseph Kussick, the radio man for recon team Flatfoot. Bell and Bock carefully placed the remains of the proud young Special Forces soldier on the poncho beside Jolly Green co-pilot Ralph Brower and Flight Engineer Eugene Clay. Although part of the mission was to recover any Americans killed in action, the discovery of the remains could bring no joy or sense of accomplishment. A noticeable pall fell over the area of operation. It was even quiet by SOG standards and they operated at a very high level of professionalism.

Only minutes passed before several of Hoepner's men caught a glimpse of two unidentified men watching the recovery detail from a vantage point above. Hoepner sent a squad to check out the spectators in hopes they were survivors watching from a rock outcropping. They were initially reported as survivors by aircraft circling the crash scene, however, the two turned out to be NVA scouts and vanished into the bush. Hoepner had instructed the squad not to follow them as they might be lead straight into an ambush. The NVA used the ambush tactic with great success and Hoepner was anxious to complete his recovery mission. It was clear the NVA was watching, and once the scouts returned to their parent unit with news of easy pickings the recovery job may get even more dangerous. The NVA may have withdrawn to a safe distance but they had not left.

Lieutenant Hoepner and Master Sergeant Fisher teamed up to search a shallow ravine, just slightly down the hill from the Jolly Green wreckage. The ravine contained some brushy vegetation and clumps of weak elephant grass. Hoepner discovered a body after only minutes in the ravine and motioned for Fisher's assistance. The body had sustained heavy damage from both the impact of the crash and the fire. Some of the clothing was still intact but there were no dog tags present. Sergeant Fisher did not need dog tags. The face was clearly that of Master Sergeant Bruce Baxter. Fisher and Baxter had soldiered together many times. Bulldog's day would become a sad one once the news was passed along. It was not the outcome they had hoped for, however, at least the families would know their loved ones were cared for and important.

Bruce Baxter had been the professional everyone had always thought him to be. His radio transmissions had remained calm and his voice steady throughout the NVA onslaught. Baxter's leadership had saved all but 2 of his team. It was a testament to his character and his skills. He had mentored Joseph Kussick and taken him under his wing. They were said to share some religious and spiritual beliefs and both were admired for their temperaments and self-restraint. The two had fought off superior NVA forces one wave after another and had miraculously made it aboard Jolly Green rescue helicopter 26. When the Air Force rescue helo received too many direct hits and crashed, the Special Forces had lost two special men; one a promising young Green Beret and the other a stellar soldier, both superior human beings.

Bulldog couldn't take anytime to mourn their losses. They pressed the search on and Sergeant First Class Bob Cavanaugh, a New Jersey native, found another body. The body lay only meters from where Baxter was found and was camouflaged with loose elephant grass and broken branches. There could be no mistake that someone had intentionally tried to hide the body. It was the final piece to the puzzle of missing crewmen from Jolly Green 26. Cavanaugh had discovered the remains of Pararescueman Sergeant Larry W. Maysey.

Maysey had made it through the Air Forces pipeline training for their elite Pararescue program. He had been in country for only a month. According to Air Force documents, Sergeant Maysey had exited the Jolly Green in a "hail of fire" to assist Kussick and Baxter get into the rescue helo's cargo bay. How Maysey managed to get Baxter and Kussick to the helo is unknown, only that he was successful in getting them aboard the ill fated chopper is known for sure. Maysey risked his life for them and they did the same for their team.

A bronze statue stands in the middle of Larry Maysey's hometown as a tribute to his selfless act of courage and his dedication to the Pararescue creed, "That others may live."

Who would have covered Maysey's body and made it more difficult to find? There was little or no mystery as to who camouflaged the Air Force P.J. By simple deduction the only possible candidate was Jolly 26's aircraft Commander Captain Gerald O. Young. He had crawled from beneath the wreckage and secured the severely injured P.J. as best he could. Badly burned and partially blinded, Captain Young could hear the voices of the NVA closing in to finish off any survivors. Hastily camouflaging Maysey, the Captain made his presence known to the NVA and led them away from the crash site. He hoped some of the crew would survive but had no way of knowing where they were or what physical shape they were in. Gaining the attention of the NVA, Young utilized his Air Force training and employed classic escape and evasion tactics. The veteran pilot took the NVA on a one mile chase off the mountain despite his own serious injuries. He hid and moved, then did it all over again through brush and treed areas, managing to keep just one move ahead of his determined pursuers. The NVA proved to be no match for the gravely wounded pilot, and when he finally heard the sound of a Huey attack helicopter he bolted from a woods line hoping to be seen.

A Marine gunship spotted Young and identified him as American. The Huey was low on fuel and power, leaving the pilot with a very difficult decision. He could try to get another helo to pick up Young if there was another helo, or risk landing and jeopardize his entire crew. The pilot set his Huey down. His crew pulled the battered Young aboard and soon they were all headed back to Khe Sanh.

Captain Gerald O. Young survived his injuries and became the only member of his crew to survive the rescue mission to Hill 891. For his bravery, resourcefulness, and ability to function under life-threatening circumstances, Captain Young was awarded the Congressional Medal of Honor. There seemed to be no shortage of bravery on or around Hill 891.

Lieutenant Hoepner's search team continued investigating the crash site and related areas on the mountainside for another hour. All the air crew members had been accounted for. The same was true for recon team Flatfoot. Unfortunately, no one had kept track of the events that unfolded on Hill 891. Information had not been shared and the fog of war continued to obscure the efforts on Hill 891.

Extra time spent searching the mountainside for something that did not exist exposed the search team unnecessarily. The NVA was still out there, as were toe poppers and the potential for any number of other injuries the mountainside could cause. There was one thing that everyone knew and was informed about and that was the weather. The mist, light rain, and fog continued its relentless effort to hamper Bulldog's effectiveness and certainly contributed to the men's psychological state. SOG operations were carried out in all types of weather. The rain was nothing new to the veteran Special Forces men who had already served numerous tours in Southeast Asia.

The effects the rain and wetness had could not be totally dismissed. At times it kept helicopters grounded, and in a more personal way it made trousers cling and rub in places that were particularly sensitive. It also softened the skin on the men's feet and promoted blisters and fungal growth. During World War I and to a lesser extent World War II, entire units were put out of action with trench foot, later renamed emersion foot. There were several preventive measures: allowing air to get to the foot, using dry socks, applying foot powder, and drying the boots. Sergeant Cavanaugh claimed to have never worn any socks at all and said his feet were always good to go. As the wet conditions continued and the mountain soaked up the rain, Hoepner's search team now faced their uphill climb with 5 bodies to take up the steep slope. Low on energy from a lack of food and sleep, it was questionable whether the team could physically get both themselves and the deceased up the hill. Sergeant First Class Ron Bock agreed that ". . . getting them out of there was going to be a chore even under peaceful, secure conditions which we soon found out we did not have."

Gerald O. Young piloted Jolly Green 26 and received
the Congressional Medal of Honor.
Sketch by Star Barkman.

The Congressional Medal of Honor. Sketch by Star Barkman.

Grave marker in Arlington Cemetery in remembrance of U.S. Air Force Pilot Captain Gerald O. Young. Photo courtesy of Colonel Rick Fuentes, N.J. State Police.

It was decided to prepare the dead Americans for a helicopter lift when the weather broke and the helos arrived. H-34 helicopters were equipped with powerful winches. They could hover, drop a line, and one of the Special Forces guys could hook the link to the already prepared bodies and the problem would be solved. There was nothing new about using a helo for winching. The Special Forces had trained for it and it was a fairly common practice. It was a reasonable alternative to carrying the bodies up the severe slope.

Jolly Green 26 Crash Site, Hill 891, 2400 hours, 10 November, 1967

The solemn task of locating and accounting for the fallen Americans was finally brought to an end by Lieutenant Rod Hoepner's group. He then organized his men for the uphill climb to the perimeter being held by the rest of Hatchet Force Bulldog. The men slipped and stumbled their way to the top. They were breathing hard when they reached their perimeter. Once on top Lieutenant Dick informed Fisher and Hoepner that the helicopter that had been requested to extract the bodies had been ordered to stand down, as the forecasters saw no opportunity to fly and darkness would be closing in. The cancellation was considered only a minor setback, since the weather had to eventually clear and the lift could take place at that time.

With all of Bulldog's elements inside their makeshift perimeter, the men took time to rehydrate on captured rain water. It would have been an excellent time to break out C-rations, even the main entre of ham and limas (a.k.a. ham and mother . . . .) would have been a welcomed meal despite the fact that they were absolutely despised by Army and Marines alike. But there were no C-rations to refill the burned calories it took to stay warm, climb mountains, and more importantly to remain alert. Bulldog could not afford to lose focus or allow fatigue to compromise their safety; after all, returning home alive was part of their mission.

Master Sergeant Fisher knew they weren't off the mountain yet and he continued to encourage each of his men to improve their positions by digging a little deeper even if it was with a knife or their bare hands. A mortar attack, rifle grenades, or a rocket propelled grenade would be disastrous without better cover. There was no substitute for self-discipline and here is where leadership and training really paid off.

RON Position, Hill 891, Laos, 1430 hours, 10 November, 1967

A commotion among the Bodes grabbed everyone's attention, including Sergeant First Class Gilbert Hamilton whose forefinger pointed down hill for all to follow. There, exiting a tree line was a platoon size group of NVA soldiers. It appeared they were about to utilize a foot trail that ran north to south. Some of Bulldog's men passed a set of binoculars around. They had been removed from an NVA corpse who had fallen victim to an A-1 Napalm strike. The binoculars were Marine Corp issue. Now back in the hands of Americans, they were trained on the unsuspecting NVA patrol. As the binoculars were passed around they could not believe their eyes. It appeared that a reddish bearded European was leading the patrol. Bizarre as it seemed it was not the first time recon teams reported seeing a suspected Russian leading a patrol. When the recon teams reported their findings it was always dismissed as over active imaginations, myth or inconsequential.

Gilbert Hamilton was not interested in being the Grand Marshall for who was the dumbest NVA patrol in Laos's parade. He viewed it as an opportunity to kill the enemy. After all, this was a war and Hamilton turned to preparing his M-60 machine gun by extending the bi pod legs and clicking them into place. The gun did not have the elevation necessary to fire over the brush, rocks, and high spots between "Hambone" and the enemy. Adapting to his problem the Sergeant spotted a stump that proved to be ideal. He raised the top cover, did a quick dusting with a paint brush and laid a belt of ammunition in the gun. He quietly closed the top cover; one of the finest weapons ever produced was good to go. Off to Hamilton's left Brooke Bell followed the same procedures Hamilton had except Bell could find nothing to elevate his M-60. Bell quickly convinced "sockless" Bob Cavanaugh to sprawl on the ground and become a human stump. Not thinking about the deafening noise produced by the M-60, Cavanaugh obliged, figuring one of Bulldog's leaders would put a halt to firing at the out of range NVA.

The NVA continued to ditty bop along the trail, totally unaware of Bulldog's presence which was a testimony to their concealment and choice of positioning, not to mention their ability to remain quiet. Lieutenant Dick had reservations about attacking the NVA who gave every indication they would walk right past Bulldog's perch on the crown of the mountain. Shooting at them might piss them off, and there was no way of telling how many men they had in the area to retaliate with, but allowing them to continue on may cause the death of other Americans or even themselves on some future mission.

Dick watched the patrol draw nearly even to Bulldog's position and he murmured to Hamilton that they were ". . . about 1,000 yards out which puts them out of effective range." Hamilton did not see it the Lieutenant's way and mouthed, "Bullshit Lieutenant they can be had." No one told Hamilton or Bell they could not engage, so when the middle of the NVA patrol passed, Hamilton opened up on them with a short burst. Then he quickly followed with another. Brook Bell's gun also went to work on the last half of the NVA patrol. The hapless NVA went into a frenzied panic. They began to drop in place. Those not hit appeared totally bewildered, giving Hamilton and Bell even more time to adjust their murderous fire. Both men were weapons experts and superior marksmen. Their attack knew no favorites and the 'Russian' himself crumpled to the ground.

This was no television show. Those on the wrong end of a speeding bullet do not hear the report of the gun before being hit. If luck is on your side and the projectile whizzed by, you may then hear the report. This NVA patrol was fresh out of luck and it took them what seemed to be an eternity to locate the muzzle flashes and the wisps of telltale smoke that leaked from the barrels of the M-60s.

Watching through the binoculars Gamble Dick could see those NVA who failed to make it to the ground were soon leveled by the two gunners. Hamilton's lips could not hide a faint smile as he looked back at Gamble Dick. There could be only two reasons for the smile; payback had been extracted for the slain Americans, or proving an officer wrong concerning his shooting skills; whichever Hambone felt vindicated.

Occasionally the NVA attempted to retrieve their dead and wounded. That proved to be a terrible mistake as each time Hamilton and Bell made the rescuers pay with their lives until all efforts completely ceased. Those who could run and crawl found cover in the woods line. It was the only place they could escape the gunner's wrath.

Master Sergeant Fisher took notice of the fleeing NVA and had worked up an 8 digit coordinate he radioed to the ever present Covey pilot who would then channel the numbers to the Air Force Command Center. The Air Force had a state of the art computer (for 1967) that could take wind speed, directions and altitude into account. They would put the data into the hands of an F-4 jet pilot so he could put bombs right on target. If the Russian-led NVA patrol was shocked by Bell and Hamilton's M-60s, they were really going to be impressed by the bombing runs that would soon be coming their way. The only drawback to finishing off the NVA patrol was if a pilot erred or if Master Sergeant Fisher somehow goofed on his 8 digit coordinates. Should either of these scenarios develop, Bulldog might receive the bombs intended for the remnants of the NVA patrol.

SOG had developed a method of summoning air assets when their teams were in dire straits by declaring on the radio a "prairie fire emergency." Should the team in peril be in Cambodia the leader could declare a "Daniel Boone emergency." Once the declaration was broadcast, pilots from any service branch flying helos, jets, or prop driven aircraft rushed to the coordinates to be available to the team in jeopardy.

Although the passing NVA patrol didn't create the proper criteria for a true prairie fire emergency, Lieutenant Dick dispensed with formalities, pressed the key on his phone and spoke the magic words. No one in the chain of command questioned the emergency request and the Air Force seemed more than ready to extract a pound of flesh from the NVA.

Only minutes passed and the Covey pilot came on Dick's radio. He instructed Bulldog to ". . . Get your heads down you'll have bombs in 30 seconds." Fisher's plan was to have bombs dropped into the woods where the NVA patrol had sought refuge from the Special Forces gunners. It would deny them the ability to regroup and stage a counter attack. The bombs would explode 1200 feet from Bulldog's position. This was closer than Air Force policy called for, although it was not unheard of. Policy was created in air-conditioned offices; reality and survival took place in the Truong Son Mountains.

The Air Force sent a pair of "fast movers" (jets) instead of the old reliable Skyraiders. When a "prairie fire emergency" was declared, any and all available aircraft made themselves available to the recon team or Hatchet Force in jeopardy. At times aircraft would stack up over the SOG team and wait their turn to deliver whatever ordnance they could dump on the NVA.

The Hatchet Force collectively sunk to the bottom of their holes waiting for the promised delivery; everyone except Sergeant Fisher who cheated a tiny peek to see the results of his math test.

Some of the men claim to have heard the jets pass overhead and some did not. There was a unanimous and affirmative vote on what they heard next. The concussion and noise shook the mountainside and rattled Bulldog's position. The explosions were "danger close" and they were followed by secondary explosions. One threw a boxcar size object hundreds of feet in the air. The pilots had hit an ammunition cache which may explain why the NVA platoon was in the vicinity of Hill 891. A light breeze blew vegetation and other matter into Bulldog's position for several minutes along with the mournful cries of the NVA wounded.

The power and violence of the bombs was a stark reminder to the Hatchet Force that those who worked in Laos and Cambodia walked a very fine line and just one miscue might be fatal. One wrong trail taken, one L.Z. left unsecured, one machine gun poorly maintained, and fate might take a terrible toll.

Master Sergeant Fisher went to the top of his class; his math and communications skills were A+ and he had eliminated the Russian-led platoon threat to Bulldog. Everyone was impressed with the air strike and the security it brought, everyone that is except Gilbert Hamilton. He felt "it could have been done by us," a feeling not shared by anyone with the possible exception of Brooke Bell. As for Lieutenant Dick, he was truly impressed with the Air Force pilots and "Top" Fisher's skills, but he continued to wonder if Bulldog had poked the proverbial stick into the hornet's nest.

<u>Hill 891, Laos, 1520 hours, 11 November, 1967</u>

With the F-4s now gone, the weapons experts began cleaning their M-60s and the rest of Bulldog worked on improving their position. There was no reason to feel secure, which prompted Hoepner, Dick and Fisher to circulate around the perimeter and encourage each team member to continue to improve his position and get their weapons clean and ammunition organized.

Just as the Hatchet Force had started to catch its collective breath shots rang out on the edge of the perimeter, one and then a second, followed by a hail of supporting fire, then quiet. Lieutenant Hoepner scrambled to where the shooting came from and caught Sergeant First

Class Ron Bock trying to get the mercenaries to cease fire, which they did.

Bock had caught a glimpse of movement in a grove of trees near where Sergeant Osborne had stepped on the mine. An NVA scout appeared, and in his haste to gather intelligence on the Hatchet Force, had unknowingly run out of cover for himself. Bock and the scout made each other out at just about the same time and both must have fought off panic as they raised their rifles intent on their own survival. Bock's AR-15 fired twice and the NVA crumpled to the ground unable to return fire. He also would not return to his unit with any helpful information about Bulldog's position. The Cambodian's volleys quickly came under control and no return fire was reported. Bock carefully made his way to the lifeless NVA scout, checked him for papers and removed his boots. The CIA could duplicate the boot soles and issue them to SOG, so tracking the recon teams would be more difficult.

Covey was made aware of this incident, and soon the ever present A-1Es were dropping Napalm on the tree area just in case the NVA were massing there for an assault.

Dick had left the PRC-25 (radio) at his own position. Upon returning he found Sergeant Hamilton in a heated debate on the radio. Dick hopped into the hole just in time to hear Hambone utter, "Fuck you bitch!" Dick's first thought was that Hambone was conversing with a certain lantern-jawed Major back at Phu Bai. "Who the hell are you talking to?" "Lieutenant, it's some Russian bitch who says we should surrender while we still can." Hamilton had less use for foreigners than his own officers, and when a woman's voice demanded surrender, Hamilton launched into a diatribe filled with a healthy dose of F-bombs.

Dick was relieved to find out the caller on the other end was not Major Snell, still he wanted to identify the mystery caller himself. The always eloquent Gilbert Hamilton turned over the handset to Dick covering the microphone and advised Dick "Don't surrender Lieutenant." Dick pressed his ring and middle finger on the send button and announced: "This is Bulldog six, who is this? Over." Astonished, a female voice immediately returned through his receiver. Hamilton had passed over the Major in question and had been conversing with a Lieutenant Colonel instead, only this was a Soviet officer. "This is Lieutenant Colonel Ludmilla Karatova" (or something like that), I am advisor to the Peoples Army of Vietnam (PAVN)." Her accent was reminiscent of

Boris Batanoff's partner Natasha of cartoon fame and the entire episode would have been amusing had it not been so dangerous. Knowing full well that the conversation should be terminated so as to deprive the NVA from using any of their directional finding equipment that came to them through the Soviet lend-lease program, Dick felt compelled to listen just a few more seconds. Ludmilla continued, "You are brave and honorable men and there is no need for you to die." "If you come to the bottom of the hill and surrender you will not be harmed and will be treated with respect." Taking a page from Hamilton's book, the Lieutenant responded with a, "Fuck you bitch, why don't you come to the top of the hill and surrender to us?" He immediately terminated the conversation and switched to another frequency. Hamilton sat on the soggy ground with a Winston clinched between his teeth and quipped, "You know Lieutenant I think you're starting to get this." It was the longest conversation the two had ever had. Was "Hambone" starting to warm up to an officer?

The mission to Hill 891 would not be the last for the odd couple, Sergeant Hamilton and Lieutenant Dick. On 14 January 1968 the two crossed the fence for one last mission. This Hatchet Force mission was sent into Laos, just south of Marine stronghold Khe Sanh to recover three bodies. Specialist 5 Gary Spann completed the trio of Special Forces guys that also included thirty three Cambodian mercenaries with the Marines supplying the helos.

Like recon team Flatfoot, recon team Indiana had been "snoopn and poopn" in Uncle Ho's neighborhood, but that was where the similarities ended. Recon team Indiana had been ambushed. They were on a plateau and the thick eight to ten foot elephant grass completely obliterated any visibility past several feet.

The hatchet force's infiltration went smoothly and they quickly located the area where recon team Indiana was operating. Dick quickly used a technique known as a clover leaf search and in a short period of time it discovered where they believed the NVA had ambushed recon team Indiana. The ambush site bore no signs of blood, little in the way of shredding from gunfire, and indications that concussion grenades had been employed. The three missing men included one American SSG Jim Cohron, U.S.A.F. and two Vietnamese who were not found. As it turned out, Sergeant Cohron was the brother-in-law of Sergeant Charles Harper who had volunteered to go on the earlier mission to Hill 891. Drag marks were followed for 100 meters and then petered out. The American searchers believed ". . . the ambush may have been a deliberate effort on the part of the NVA to take prisoners."

The Lieutenant began to move his men to a position that offered more cover, better visibility, and a closer L.Z. for the helos. Still there had been no FAC flying over his men, and unbeknownst to him, there would not be a FAC for the duration. A FAC had been readied from Khe Sanh but crashed on takeoff killing both men aboard. Those men were Air Force Captain and pilot of the aircraft, Sam Beach and his covey rider, SFC Dan Chaney. Whether they crashed on takeoff or were shot down was unclear. What was clear was that their absence was yet another tragedy for two more families back home. Also, the Hatchet Force was in peril and in desperate need of the Covey Fac. The death of Captain Beach and SFC Chaney also lead to speculation that the missing name of the pilot who flew so courageously over Hill 891 could have been Sam Beach, now and forever silenced by the crash. There would be no air cover, and no artillery support, because as always, helos were overwhelmed by demand. Moving thirty-six men through the elephant grass, no matter how much care was taken, created unnatural movement in the grass. Knowing the movement might catch the eye of the NVA, Dick deemed it necessary to send a small detail (six men) to secure their rear. The tactics were right out of a small unit tactics handbook. It came as no surprise that S.F.C. Gilbert Hamilton and Specialist 5 Gary Spann volunteered to take four Bodes and make sure the NVA weren't going to attack the Hatchet Force from behind while they moved to a better position.

Hamilton had trained some of these Cambodians, and they had a mutual admiration for each other. Four quickly joined the two Americans and began to wade into the sea of elephant grass. The distance between the rear guard and primary body grew to fifty meters when suddenly a heavy volume of AK-47 fire erupted. Instantly, cries of pain rang out. All six had been hit. S.F.C. Hamilton had been hit in the abdomen, Spann in the jaw, and two indigenous KIA and two wounded. At about the same time the primary group of the Hatchet Force also was taken under fire by the NVA.

Contact between the rear guard and the primary force temporarily ceased as Hamilton slipped into a state of unconsciousness. Gary Spann instinctively tried to pick up the reins of leadership, but his wound prevented him from being understood. Somehow Hamilton rallied from his unconscious state and was able to pop a smoke grenade requested by Gamble Dick. Once the rear guard's position was established, Dick organized his men on line and assaulted the area Hamilton's attackers were thought to be in. Firing on semi-auto from the hip, Dick's group quickly neutralized the ambushers in only five minutes, but it was already too late for two of the Cambodians. The assault also produced two NVA prisoners. However, in the confusion the Cambodians killed both in retribution for killing their friends. When a lull in the action allowed, Lieutenant Dick inspected the two NVA. He noticed two things immediately: (1) they were both very dead and (2) they were both equipped with brand spanking new gear. In law enforcement this could be called a clue. Clues were exactly what SOG was gathering for the CIA and quite a price in blood was being exchanged for it.

One clue alone was meaningless but by 1968 many reports had been submitted to Colby's gang. Two huge game changers were in the NVA's plans and they were looming and creeping closer every day. One was the massive TET offensive set to explode at the end of the month and the other was the Marines being put under siege at Khe Sanh.

Gamble Dick did not have time to analyze the big picture or the future moves of the NVA. He had radioed for helos and the Marines responded by sending a flight of H34s for the exfiltration. Before they could land one H-34 was hosed down by an automatic weapon, the door gunner killed and the helo limped off towards Khe Sanh. The rest of the aircraft picked up the wounded and the living until the final chopper was loaded. The pilot was unable to get the last helo off the ground. It bobbed up and down, groaned but it would not take off. One of the Bodes was forced out and Lieutenant Dick quickly jumped out also fearing the mercenary would be left for the NVA to savage. The helo lifted off now that the extra baggage had been off-loaded. Too much weight plus A.D.F. (altitude density factor) had made orphans of the two final members of the Hatchet Force. Dick gathered up his one remaining charge and made for a safer place, he hoped. Moving only a short distance two NVA popped out of the grass and attempted to train the muzzles of their rifle barrels on the Special Forces Lieutenant. The end result of this encounter Lieutenant 2, NVA 0. The Marines had not forgotten Dick and his Bode, and when the Marine helo dove to their position, they launched themselves through the open door. Once in the air, the crew chief removed his glove and reached into his flight suit producing a red and black package of Lucky Strike cigarettes. He drew one out with the dexterity of a veteran degenerate smoker. He put it to his lips and fired it up with his genuine U.S.M.C. lighter. He then handed it to Gamble Dick, who with hand shaking and heart pounding, smoked his first and last cancer stick to the very last puff. According to Gamble Dick "I never smoked another cigarette since because I don't think any other cigarette could ever taste as good."

Several days following the exfiltration, Sergeant First Class Gilbert Lee Hamilton succumbed to his wounds. The native of Colorado was awarded the Distinguished Service Cross for his bravery and tenacity. Sadly, it was awarded posthumously. By volunteering to cover the Hatchet Force's back trail many lives were saved. S.F.C. Hamilton's name can be found on the Vietnam Memorial Wall on Panel 36E line 073.

SOG teams brought back from their missions a wealth of information regarding activity on the Ho Chi Minh Trail. They reported on massive truck convoys traveling from North to South, provided intel on anti-aircraft guns being towed southward, and troop movements complete with statistics. They submitted reports on Europeans leading NVA patrols and provided eye witness accounts of the same. In some instances, photographs were submitted and NVA tank treads were reported. SOG radios had received amateurish psy-ops delivered by women with Russian accents and the list continued. SOG men even snatched an occasional prisoner for interrogation purposes.

However, when SOG leaders were interviewed in Saigon by William Colby's officials, there seemed to be a lack of interest, almost as if it had little importance. Just what and how much of the intelligence was utilized was impossible to determine. However, the attitude in Saigon left some SOG field leaders questioning the worthiness of their very costly excursions into Uncle Ho's neighborhood.

At least some of SOG's leaders became suspicious and believed they were being used as bait to entice the NVA to amass and by doing so provide more productive targets for American aircraft. At least one Covey pilot dreaded supporting SOG operations into Laos and referred to them as "suicide missions" with less than a good chance to succeed. Most of these sentiments were never voiced or felt until long after the war ended. SOG continued to actively operate into the fall of 1971. Those who soldiered for SOG were totally dedicated to one another regardless of their feelings. So thoroughly professional were the SOG men that at one point they were killing 150 NVA to every Green Beret lost as noted by

Major John L. Plaster in his book, <u>SOG</u>. They were true commandos, a term used far too often but certainly earned by the men of SOG.

Less than an hour after Ludmilla's social call the unmistakable sound of a mortar round touching down outside of Bulldog's perimeter sent the men scrambling for cover. The mortar seemed to come from Bulldog's southeast and travelled directly over their heads, crashed on the ground, exploded and sent shrapnel and dirt flying in every direction.

The jagged pieces of shrapnel came in every size and shape as a result of the mortar's explosion. Human tissue stood no chance versus the razor sharp steel pieces. The wounds received as a result of flying shrapnel were often gaping and promoted large quantities of blood loss which in turn required medical treatment immediately.

The initial blast was followed by another and the second by three more. Mortar attacks often raised the curtain for an infantry attack. Was Bulldog in for the fight of their lives? Mortar rounds are normally fired with a trajectory and are most effective when the mortar team has a forward observer to "adjust" the strike of the round so as to increase or decrease the range where the round lands. The NVA gunners were unable to walk their rounds into Bulldog's position and no one was injured.

The Hatchet Force had been spared. They had utilized their holes to stay low and avoid any deadly shrapnel that indiscriminately maim and kill their targets. It was indeed a blessing the NVA had not sent their best marksmen. During the attack one brave soul ventured out of his hole and sprawled on top of a previously wounded Cambodian shielding him from further damage. Special Forces Sergeant First Class Ron Bock had already played a major role earlier in the mission and had come up big once again.

Covey returned to Dick's radio advising they use an alternate frequency when Dick responded, "FAC wanted to know what happened down there?" Covey was advised about the mortar attack and Ludmilla's surrender demand. There was a long pause while Covey relayed Bulldog's message back to Forward Operating Base #1 in Phu Bai. When Covey returned to the radio, Phu Bai chose to ignore the Ludmilla story. Maybe a short chat with Hambone would have been more convincing.

Covey had some good news to deliver Bulldog. The weather was supposed to break during the night and helos would be inbound to extract Bulldog early A.M. The Covey pilots were truly a God-send to SOG teams in the field. It appeared the hits just kept on coming for

Bulldog when the "Bodes" take out order arrived in the form of some nice plump grubs served over a bed of rotting log; apparently the worm had definitely turned for Bulldog.

Still another long, wet and cold night lay ahead, a night without significant nourishment. What would the NVA have in store for Bulldog following their unsuccessful mortar attack?

Ron "Doc" Bock—On Hill 891 he called on all his cross training for a successful conclusion. Sketch by Star Barkman.

CHAPTER 12

THAT'S A NEGATIVE

<u>Hill 891, Laos, 2100 hours, 10 November, 1967</u>

As dusk arrived, the Hatchet Force crawled back into their positions for what they hoped would be their final night on Hill 891 in the Truong Son Mountains. Stay alive for a few more hours and Bulldog could claim to have successfully "cleaned up the mess," depending on how you looked at it.

Total darkness had not quite taken hold when a filthy Bruce Lutrell slithered into Gamble Dick's fighting position with arm extended and palm up. "Try this sir." The Lieutenant saw a tiny green pill sitting on top of a filthy, unwashed hand. "A breath mint? We don't have a single square of toilet paper among us and you want to share a breath mint?" "No sir, it's a Green Hornet. It will help you stay awake." The Lieutenant popped the pill and swallowed. Lutrell wished him "bon appétit".

Bruce Lutrell was a "Maine Man," a phrase coined during the Civil War as a tribute to the high character of Maine's fighting men. Rising to the rank of Master Sergeant, Lutrell was obviously cut from the same cloth as were Maine's Gettysburg heroes. Known as a risk taker, he was able to mix in just enough self-control to be an effective Special Forces leader in the field.

It would be fair to say Bruce Lutrell and Lloyd Fisher appeared to have attended totally different Special Forces schools and training, but in fact, they had received nearly the exact training courses. The difference between them was their personalities and their interpretation of soldiering.

Lutrell was said to be an outstanding trainer of Special Forces men and also a great charismatic leader. Yet, while in the field, Bruce Lutrell walked a fine line between bold and reckless. Although the Sergeant's methods brought him notoriety and success, he was killed in action less than two years after serving up Lieutenant Dick's "breath mint," SFC Lutrell had been serving with a MIKE force at the time inside Vietnam. He had been killed by NVA shrapnel while working on a plan of action with Special Forces legend, Billy Waugh. The sad event was noted by Waugh in his <u>Thoughts from Special Forces Days</u>. Bruce Lutrell's name can be found at the Vietnam Veteran's Memorial in Washington, DC on panel 24W, line 60. Master Sergeant Lutrell left a young wife. This was a theme repeated all too often by those working for SOG and the Special Forces in general.

Lloyd Fisher soon showed up at Lieutenant Dick's position. He wanted to discuss how the remains would be removed and where the all important P.Z. (pick up zone) was going to be for the morning extraction. In addition, Fisher requested Dick to radio for an H-34 helicopter that was equipped with a powerful winch so the KIA (killed in action) could be lifted from the mountainside into the helo's cargo hold, taken for positive identification, and returned to their loved ones in the States. The H-34 would have to come to a hover and send a line to the ground. Because the helo would be vulnerable, two gun ships would be necessary for its security. Fisher also wanted Dick to know that Bulldog would have to send some men to secure the winch line and provide their own security. The entire operation should take less than 15 minutes plus the travel time. The primary force would have to hump it west and secure the P.Z. so the helicopters could land safely, get Bulldog on board, and return to F.O.B. #1 at Phu Bai. The coordination would be critical. The helos would not want to spend any unnecessary time sitting in the pick-up zone.

Fisher and Dick shared the same position inside their perimeter once again. They also shared a wish that this would be the final night on the mountain. They alternated making rounds to each of the Hatchet Forces' positions, leaving the other to monitor the all important radio. Some positive signs began to show in the night sky. The clouds were now giving way to an occasional show of stars. Then an old friend's voice came on the radio. It was Blind Bat 03, whose engine noise had betrayed them long before Bulldog's radio came to life. "Bats" presence would send a message to the NVA that Bulldog was not alone. The voice, that reassuring "we have your back voice," gave a psychological boost to Bulldog's leaders once again and the positive vibe was passed on through the entire team. Positive vibes were helpful, but they couldn't dry wet feet, clean filthy uniforms, or fill empty stomachs; nor could they make the fear of an NVA assault go away.

Fisher advised Blind Bat to hold on to their light show unless Bulldog made contact with the enemy. Blind Bat responded "Roger your request." The team waged a mighty battle, not with the NVA but a fight against fatigue, exhaustion, and the effects of sleep deprivation. Only self-discipline, training, and fear could keep the men awake and make survival possible. Bruce Lutrell's pharmaceutical answer to remaining awake, the Green Hornet, turned out to be ". . . worthless as tits on a canary."

The radio crackled once again. It was Alley Cat and the voice from the "Cat" belonged to the Airborne battlefield Commander. His message was simple; Bulldog did not have to worry ". . . we will have you out at first light." The Commander had beau coup (many) assets including Skyraiders, choppers, and F-4s all lined up for an early morning extraction. The Commander also guaranteed his personal vigilance throughout the night. Things were looking up for the Hatchet Force.

As powerful an ally as the battlefield Commander was, no one could order the night to pass any faster and the occasional radio check brought little relief to the monotony. The real attack was launched not by the NVA but by the "sandman" who made every effort to get each man to succumb to sleep. Sergeant Lutrell's Green Hornet never took effect. Darkness begrudgingly released its hold on Hill 891 as did the rain and mist. Weak rays of sun began to filter downward. For the first time in days the weather allied itself with Bulldog and a promising conclusion to the mission could be felt throughout the Hatchet Force.

Master Sergeant Fisher had selected his group of men to descend the slope and attach the remains to the winch line of the H-34 helo. The task would be a physical and emotional challenge, and should the NVA choose to ambush the patrol, the entire plan would have to be revised. Should the NVA decide to take down more helicopters, and that was a possibility, Hill 891 would experience even more chaos and the search and rescue mission would take on even greater consequences. There could be no denying there was risk involved in the plan to recover the American remains now resting on Hill 891.

Hill 891, Laos, 0750 hours, 11 November, 1967

Lieutenant Dick watched as Sergeant Fisher and his detail started their descent so as to close the deal on Hill 891. It has long been a military tradition to return the fallen to their families. It was the least that could be done. It was a noble tradition, yet it also put others at risk, and in every war the number of KIA increased because of it.

The main body of Bulldog began their trek to secure the landing zone so their transport helos could land in safety and take on the Hatchet Force. A short time passed and Covey pilot "Kip" Kippenhan flew directly over Bulldog's primary group. Dick's radio came alive. "Bulldog, Bulldog, do you read?" "Go ahead Covey, this is Bulldog." "The helos are on route, the E.T.A. is 20 minutes. Will the P.Z. be secure?"

Dick realized the advisement had left out any mention of the all important H-34 for winching and the two gunships. He ignored the question regarding the P.Z. security and asked for the ETA for the H-34 and gunships. Covey came back, "Bulldog leader, that's a negative on the H-34 and the gunships. They want you out now! They will not hover a helicopter in this area, move your team to the P.Z. and recall the detail heading down hill."

Gamble Dick could not believe what he was hearing. American remains were going to be abandoned on a hillside in Laos? He once again requested Covey to send an H-34 and this time Covey was more forceful with a loud "Negative!"

The Lieutenant realized he had a dilemma on his hands. Not being able to get an H-34 made it appear he wasn't forceful with those in command. However, if he argued too hard and more men were killed removing the remains, he could be facing some serious repercussions with those high in the chain of command. It was unlikely the detail sent down hill could physically carry the five bodies to the pick-up zone. That would require a Herculean effort even for well-rested and well-fed men. Even if the detail could carry the remains, 20 minutes would not be enough time for them to rendezvous with the helos. The Lieutenant was in the "rocking chair" and he knew it.

The dye had been cast maybe at Phu Bai or Da Nang; maybe it was the Airborne Battlefield Commander, somewhere in between or higher. Lieutenant Dick did not have the luxury of debating or questioning the whys and why nots of the failure to send an H-34. With men's lives still very much at risk, not only those of the Hatchet Force but the crew of the incoming helos as well, it was a done deal. Second guessing would only consume precious time. There were decisions to be made on behalf of the living. The decision to pull the plug on the mission and leave the remains of Baxter, Kussick, Brower, Clay, and Maysey would have long lasting effects well beyond anyone's comprehension on that sunny morning on Hill 891.

The Airborne Commander had promised assets and true to his word, four A-1E Skyraiders appeared on station over the battlefield, courtesy of the United States Air Force stationed at Udorn Royal Tai Air Base. Dick requested two of the Sandies work over the P.Z. where the helicopters would soon land. The other two Sandies were directed by Dick to drop their ordnance on a stand of trees where Ron Bock had engaged and shot an NVA soldier. To mark Bulldog's position, the Hatchet Force stretched out a day-glow orange panel showing Bulldog's perimeter line to the west of where the strike was requested. Once again, the strike would be "danger close" to the Hatchet Force's perimeter. It required absolute confidence in the professionalism of the A1-E pilots. That confidence was well founded; "ground pounders" from Korea to Vietnam had depended on A1-E pilots and their versatile aircraft. The propeller-driven dinosaur was not as sleek or sexy as the jets being used in Vietnam, but they could pack large amounts of rockets, Napalm, and cannons. It flew at relatively low speeds, which invited the NVA to shoot at it with whatever weapon they had available. The NVA hated both the aircraft and the pilots who had a reputation for risk-taking and were considered to be World War II throwbacks. They seemed to cultivate their reputation. Some of the pilots had switched over to the A1-Es from other aircraft to become more involved in combat assignments. They never seemed to disappoint the men on the ground.

The U.S.A.F. A1-E Skyraider relentlessly pursued
the NVA in the Southeast Asia theatre.
Sketch by Star Barkman.

U.S. Air Force Skyraider supports a Hatchet Force working in Laos.
Sketch by Gamble Dick.

The Commander of the two Sandies was Major Robert Aycock who rolled his Sandy in from the east, streaked over the perimeter and released 2 silver canisters of napalm. Napalm was jellied gasoline. It exploded on contact, sucked the oxygen out of the air depriving the lungs of what they most needed, and proceeded to burn everything it came in contact with. Napalm had been around since 1943. Dr. Louis Feiser was the inventor. He also laid claim to life saving research in cancer, blood clotting, and malaria. American college students chose to protest Napalm's use. Led by off campus anti-war activists, they pounced on Dow Chemical, the manufacturer of Napalm. The protesters never succeeded in getting either Dr. Feiser or Dow Chemical to back down, and an ample supply was always present in Vietnam.

The use of napalm was judged to be a dirty trick and an instrument of a corrupt and morally bankrupt society. Burned and melted flesh had impact and offended the senses while an R.P.G. fragment to the chest seemed more acceptable.

In June of 1972, a famous picture taken by Nick Ut hit the newsstands in the U.S. The photo showed a nine year old girl, Kim Phuc, fleeing her village following a napalm strike mistakenly dropped by a South Vietnamese pilot. The girl was horribly burned and the photograph turned out to be worth far more than a thousand words.

Conspicuously absent in the news were atrocities committed intentionally by the VC and NVA at the city of Hue where 3,500 South Vietnamese civilians were summarily executed.

The point being, that all atrocities should be exposed, investigated and the perpetrators punished, not just crimes selected for propaganda purposes. Vietnam had its share of atrocities, brutalities and friendly fire. What war didn't?

Major Aycock's wingman followed in his path and also released 2 canisters. The four silver barrels hurtled like bowling balls down a lane and found their target in the woods line just about where Ron Bock had faced off with an NVA scout.

With four flashes, one succeeding the other, the jungle foliage lit up. The pilot's marksmanship had been superb. All of the Napalm found its mark. Ron Bock gave this appraisal. "Lieutenant Dick called for the Napalm strike into the woods line, and it was much appreciated not only for the security it provided but also for the heat it generated on that cold, damp morning."

Satisfied the enemy could not have survived the Napalm strike, Dick began the main body's movement to the pick-up zone. On their way only a couple of minutes, the lifting detail Fisher had sent down hill caught up to the main body of the Hatchet Force. Realizing the remains were being left on the mountainside sent Top Fisher, at top speed, straight up hill until he found Lieutenant Dick. The Master Sergeant was slightly out of breath when he closed on the Lieutenant. Dick already knew what was on Fisher's mind. Being out of breath and in a hurry was uncharacteristic for Fisher and gave away the fact the veteran Special Forces sergeant was very unhappy, which was a state he seldom visited. He wasted no time voicing his disgust and disappointment, loudly proclaiming "We didn't finish the friggin mission." Dick did not respond and continued humping up the hill but Fisher again persisted. "We didn't finish it Lieutenant." This time Dick responded. "Top, it wasn't my call to make. I wasn't given a choice. They don't want to hover a helicopter down there and I can't say I blame them. They want us out right now." His voice trailed off and Fisher seemed to read the situation for what it was, a Catch-22. What if A1-E pilot Major Jimmy Kilborne's theory of a flak trap was correct and they were waiting for another helicopter to blow up and more crewmen to kill?

Exactly what motivated the decision to hold the H-34? Was the decision made to spare the lives of more crewmen and prevent the loss of another helicopter? Or were they afraid the mission was spinning out of control and somehow would be exposed to the American public?

The effect of not recovering the American KIAs was felt most by their families. That empty feeling continues to this day. As for those involved in a rescue that risked their lives and withstood the hardships the mission dealt, they felt the H-34 was a reasonable and feasible method to bring the Americans out of Laos. Some of Bulldog's men felt they did everything possible, and although they came up short, they had accomplished a great deal. Other members have wrestled with an empty feeling because they hadn't completed ". . . the friggin mission."

Bulldog made it to the pick-up zone without further incident. They secured the zone where the A1-Es had released their Napalm. The choppers landed and loaded the Hatchet Force with only a few poorly placed pot shots taken at the helos on their departure. The lack of a concerted NVA effort at the pick up zone may well be credited to the Air Force A1-Es, or to the NVA's desire not to tangle with them again.

The Cambodian mercenary that had been injured earlier was loaded on the first helo out and thanks to Ron Bock survived after further treatment at Phu Bai Hospital. The last boots to step off Hill 891 were filled by Lieutenant Dick. The mission was officially over, but it wasn't really over, not by a long shot.

CHAPTER 13

STEAK AND EGGS

FOB#1, SVN, 0800, 11 November, 1967

The poorly aimed pot shots the NVA took at the departing choppers seemed like nothing more than a slight inconvenience to men who had been subjected to much greater threats to their well-being. In less than an hour the wet and cold would vanish, as had Ludmilla and Red Beard, he was of course gone forever. The helos touched down on that same dusty, weed-infested landing zone at Forward Operating Base #1 at Phu Bai. The Hatchet Force moved on feet that seemed to have concrete blocks lashed to them. They peeled off what remained of their fatigues and made their way to the showers. Phu Bai was home, and what a place to call home.

The Mess Sergeant got busy preparing the traditional steak and eggs dinner that each returning recon team and Hatchet Force was treated to. It was a kind of Thanksgiving of sorts. Bulldog had been without food for over 70 hours, unless the peach halves, plump grubs and the Slim Jims Cavanaugh brought qualified as meals. The steak and eggs came out in waves and was consumed in great quantities. As predicted the hunger, wet, and cold began its journey into the memory of those who participated on Hill 891. However, as the physical discomforts seemed to fade, the recollection of the five Americans left behind made its presence felt. As good as the Mess Sergeant at Phu Bai was, he could not make the remains on the ponchos disappear. That memory would revisit the men of Hatchet Force Bulldog many times. For some it continues to visit them often.

There was an informal debriefing that followed each mission to keep the camp commander informed and lay out the basics of what transpired in the field. A formal debriefing was to be held the following day in Saigon. That session would be conducted by Colby's boys and only Lieutenant Dick would be required to attend. Until then some much needed sleep was in order. All of the men seemed to take advantage of the rack time except the Lieutenant. For him sleep would not come. Sergeant Lutrell's Green Hornet must have had a delayed fuse and he was now hopelessly wide awake. Dick remained awake all night and had no trouble making his flight to Saigon in the morning.

Colby's interrogators in Saigon debriefed recon teams and Hatchet Force leaders after each mission into Laos and Cambodia to glean information. The information obtained from these missions was the exact reason for sending the teams into Uncle Ho's neighborhood. The Lieutenant had his thoughts and information organized and he was prepared to share the intel with the C.I.A.

Still wide awake when he stepped on board the Huey for the trip to Saigon, Dick was as ready as he could be for his first debrief at MAC-V Headquarters.

Recon teams, and to a lesser extent Hatchet Forces, returned from their missions with specific intelligence concerning the NVA presence on and around the Ho Chi Minh Trail. Colby's Remington Raiders would then put all the specifics together and a big picture would come into focus. Americans would risk their lives, some would become permanently injured, and some would never return in an effort to supply the CIA with information that could save other American lives. The Ho Chi Minh Trail was vital to the North's war effort, and according to John L. Plaster, by the end of 1967, NVA forces in Laos and Cambodia had climbed to above 100,000 with 40,000 of them detailed as Ho Chi Minh Trail security. In that year alone, 100,000 NVA passed down the Trail. SOG typically fielded 30 or 40 Americans at once in Laos and Cambodia. "Finally by late 1967 nearly every other SOG cross border mission made contact with about half the contacts leading to live or die shootouts against a vastly more numerous enemy."

Like all those who brought their team's mission information to Colby, Gamble Dick entered the debriefing with a high attitude certain that Bulldog's mission was worthy and would contribute to SOG's behind the line efforts.

Two interrogators met Dick at the office door. One wore a major's insignia on the collar of his starched and Khaki uniform. The other had his tennis outfit on, complete with crew socks and some sort of club insignia on the chest. There was arrogance about the two and there was an assembly line feeling like this isn't all that important, let's get it done. Maybe the interview was cutting into court time or an important tournament.

Early in the interview Dick was allowed to give a short narrative describing what took place on Hill 891. He began by describing the endless number of Chinese trucks they had observed, undoubtedly on their way to South Vietnam via the Ho Chi Minh Trail. He also explained how Sergeant Gilbert Hamilton engineered a long range ambush on a patrol led by what appeared to be a European and the bizarre conversation with the heavily accented Ludmilla. He conveyed the insignificant strategic value of Hill 891, the tenacity the NVA displayed in the immediate vicinity, and how many NVA lives were likely taken by our gunships, Skyraiders, and the combination of Sergeant Bell and Sergeant Hamilton. He concluded by explaining the loss of American lives, Ozzy's serious injury and Zanow and Woolridge's brush with death, not to mention the massive effort put forth during the rescue operation. It all seemed to add up and point to something, but what? Connecting the dots was Colby's mission. His starched and pressed interviewers couldn't last a minute in the jungle, and worse yet, they didn't seem interested in the dots, let alone connecting them.

Dick quickly found himself being ushered unceremoniously to the door, interview completed. There had been no acknowledgement for a job well done or affirmation that the mission had provided information that was useable and worthwhile. There wasn't even a sorry for the loss of Bruce Baxter, Joseph Kussick, Ralph Brower, Eugene Clay, Bill Whitney or Larry Maysey. Apparently Colby's little lemmings had heard enough, and Dick was cut loose to sample Saigon's well stocked liquor supply, pathetic live rock bands, and the copious amount of bargain basement sex available everywhere.

Placing MAC-V in Saigon may have been an Army conspiracy, but that would have been giving them credit for an awful lot of planning. Saigon had turned into a cesspool, but it did provide an opportunity for those with monstrous memories to wash them away with cheap thrills, if only for a short time.

The intelligence collected by SOG teams had been paid for in blood, time, and taxpayer's money. Day in and day out, SOG teams sweated, shivered, and suffered casualties all for the sake of accumulating intelligence. Where did it all go and did it serve a purpose worthy of the men collecting it? Army and Air Force air crews shot down and killed on a mountain top, Special Forces guys killed and maimed, scores of NVA trucks heading south, European advisors leading NVA patrols, and Russian advisors plying third grade psy-ops all were seemingly ignored. Maybe Colby's guys thought Hill 891 was nothing more than the overactive imagination of an inexperienced First Lieutenant or that Russians being involved was too politically charged. Maybe he was trying to feather his own nest, come off as a hero, or trying to pin on Captain's bars. Maybe Dick just misread his two interviewers.

Maybe Colby's guys had heard the same stories over and over again and just became bored, or maybe they thought the whole thing was just bullshit. If MAC V was just screwing with Dick's mind they had succeeded. He stepped on to that Saigon street with questions he could not answer.

Gamble Dick thought the request by the Russian Lieutenant Colonel to surrender a childish and baseless joke. Yet two of his own countrymen were able to force surrender from the promising young Special Forces officer. He did not give up his rifle, sign any papers, or raise his hands over his head. Instead of giving up his .45, he gave away his naiveté, not to the NVA but to a couple of office stooges. They probably didn't even know they were taking it.

Working in an air-conditioned office, wearing starched and pressed uniforms and playing tennis, these guys could afford to be blasé. SOG men could not afford to become apathetic. They had to "cross the fence," hump more mountains, and confront the NVA in their own backyard.

Dick only surrendered his naiveté. He now had to battle the cheap booze and emaciated "Boom Boom girls" in Saigon. The experience had been surreal from the interviewer's tennis togs to the ridiculous platform shoes worn by the bar flies. An ocean of Jack Daniels couldn't change the outcome of the mission to Hill 891. What Gamble Dick needed was someone he could trust. Saigon was the last place to locate trust.

Dick hitched a ride back to Phu Bai on an Army Huey. The noise from the rotor and engine was intense, yet he could still hear Lloyd

Fisher's words. "We didn't finish the friggin mission." Those words rattled around like a BB in a boxcar. It may not have been one of Top Fisher's most eloquent statements, but his words cut right to the chase. The mission on Hill 891 was not only unfinished, but it would never end or so it seemed.

Hill 891, Laos, 15-17 November, 1967

During the week that followed their homecoming steak and eggs dinner, two separate opportunities presented themselves to revisit the crash site. The purpose was to recover the Americans KIA and presumably still on Hill 891. The first attempt was met by a thick wall of fog and was obvious to Master Sergeant Lloyd Fisher that a thumbs down had to be given to the mission. The VNAF helicopters and all aboard were much relieved when their H-34s pulled away from Hill 891 and departed the soupy mixture surrounding the 1,000 foot plus elevation. It was reported that the mountain could not be seen.

Within 48 hours of their return the VNAF again agreed to fly remnants of Bulldog back to Hill 891. This time the weather was far more cooperative and it promised to be a day that would allow "the friggin mission" to be completed.

As the H-34s cruised over the crash site and battlefield, the lead helo reported seeing people on the mountainside. It was never established if these were Laotians, NVA soldiers, or other indigenous peoples. The mission was prematurely scrubbed via the radio. The order is said to have come from Da Nang. Some believed that the order to abort came from Master Sergeant Billy Waugh. Waugh may well have been the best known of all SOG men. His missions were the topics of discussions throughout the SOG community. They often reached the status of sagas and Waugh himself reached legendary status and became a Sergeant Major. It was said that Waugh had caught wind of a flak trap once again being employed by the NVA on Hill 891, and he had enough juice to pull the plug on the recovery effort, thus saving the lives of those aboard the H-34s. Billy Waugh's involvement could not be verified, however, the mission was definitely aborted and once again the recovery of remains had been stymied.

The days turned into weeks and some of the men left for other assignments. Most of Bulldog's men would soldier on with other reconnaissance teams and Hatchet Forces. They would continue to serve with the fine professionals SOG had blended together. They would reenter Laos on more dangerous missions. Some, like the hard charging Gilbert Hamilton and Bruce Lutrell, would make the ultimate sacrifice behind enemy lines. The secret war would report their deaths as having occurred while serving inside South Vietnam and few details were offered. Those who survived and returned home often found their hearts and minds drifting back to the men left on Hill 891. For those whose boots had trudged over the mountain, and those who flew above it, Hill 891 remained in their psyche. There was more to come regarding Hill 891, some sooner, some later, and some much later. No one realized what was in the very near future lurking just over the next mountain or around the next bend in the trail. Any plans to return to Hill 891 would be interrupted by the TET offensive. FOB #1 would be hit by a rocket attack, S.F. bases would be overrun by NVA tanks, and demands on Special Forces would supersede any undone business.

The mess sergeant's steak and eggs was always a huge morale booster and they filled the empty stomachs each and every time served. But, "that empty feeling" remained in their hearts and that hunger could never be relieved.

CHAPTER 14

DE' JA VU ALL OVER AGAIN

Hill 891, Laos, Southeast Asia, 2003

In July of 2003 two of Hatchet Force Bulldog's most prominent members returned to Southeast Asia and into the Truong Son Mountains. For former Special Forces Sergeants Lloyd Fisher and Ron Bock, 36 years had passed since they had been exfiltrated from Hill 891 by Marine helicopters and delivered back to Forward Operating Base #1 at Phu Bai. The remains of their countrymen did not accompany them.

This was an opportunity for the two former SOG members to turn the page on their long past mission to Hill 891 in Laos. To the highly competitive and driven Lloyd Fisher and to Ron Bock as well, this trip would provide the means to complete the mission they had started 36 years ago. Now into their 60s (Bock) and 70s (Fisher), the two had once again been recruited. This time around it would not be the United States Army, Special Forces, or Studies and Observation Group doing the recruiting. This mission into Laos would not be planned by a Major, Lieutenant or Colonel. Instead a doctor would take the lead. Her name was Dr. Joan E. Baker. She was a forensic anthropologist. A civilian employee with the Army's Central Identification Laboratory in Hawaii, she would double as a recruiter.

The CIL group was the scientific arm of JPAC formed to bring answers to families whose loved ones had never returned from America's longest war, Vietnam. Baker had previously been to Hill 891 as had other anthropologists. It was there they began a search for the remains of

Joseph Kussick, Bruce Baxter, Larry Maysey, Ralph Brower, and Eugene Clay. The early site work was promising but did not produce any remains. This was the sole purpose of the mission.

Prior to the return trip to Laos, Dr. Baker had been contacted by two men who offered a suggestion regarding the recovery of remains on Hill 891. The men were Air Force veterans Jeff Nash and Jack McTasney. Nash had served 21 years in the Air Force and had worn the Larry Maysey bracelet since hearing of his loss. Jack McTasney was the same Jolly Green pilot that miraculously flew his rescue helo off Hill 891 and back to safety with both his crew and a part of Recon Team Flatfoot. It was those two men that supplied Baker with the names of Lloyd Fisher and Ron Bock in hopes they might be of assistance in locating the remains.

Being the consummate professional, Dr. Baker quickly contacted and recruited the two former Special Forces and SOG commandos to return with JPAC to Hill 891, this time as advisors. Although the 36 years had claimed their superior physical conditioning, both had maintained a robust lifestyle and were more than capable for this mission. While their strength and flexibility could not match the high watermark it reached during their stint with Special Forces, they were in remarkable condition and very eager to advise the JPAC team in hopes of bringing the new mission to a productive conclusion.

The two SOG men had logged many miles via helicopter during their Special Forces and Army days, mostly in Hueys and H-34s. This time they would fly in a light observation helo to recon Hill 891 once again. The helo pilot approached the mountain much the same way as it had been done in 1967, only with far less stress and forebodings.

As the mountainside approached, the memories and geographical anomalies began to kick in. The tree lines, wash or ravine, rock croppings, steep slopes, and crest were all recognized. They pointed to clearings and their RON (remain overnight) positions. Their heads moved up and down in agreement to the location of events that they could never forget even had they wanted to.

There were also some conspicuous things absent that weren't missed at all. There was no smoke rising from the wrecked helos, no smell of napalm or cordite, and no sweat on their hands as a result of nerves. The NVA had lifted their flak trap and moved on, probably to fight at the siege of Khe Sanh to kill or be killed during the TET offensive.

Why was this final mission necessary? Was the NVA the primary hurdle to the combined search and rescue effort and their inability to finish "the friggin mission?"

By 1967, the NVA had developed into a well-trained and professionally equipped fighting force. The Soviets had invested heavily in the North Vietnamese Army as down payment for the military goodies. The North had only to surrender their political souls. The Chinese also contributed to Ho Chi Minh's quest to unite North and South Vietnam under the Communist umbrella. Other Soviet bloc countries such as Czechoslovakia were also encouraged by the Soviets to make a contribution to the fledgling Communists. As a result, weapons of war such as AK-47 rifles flowed like water into the capable hands of the Northerners. Rifles were not their only gifts. Chinese trucks like the ones observed by Bulldog rumbled down the Ho Chi Minh Trail in a never ending convoy delivering their lethal payloads of men and munitions. As time moved on the NVA's arsenal of weapons grew to include tanks, field artillery, and even sophisticated anti-aircraft missiles. Not bad for a peasant army.

Another factor that played into the hands of the NVA (in addition to weapons) was time and casualties. Neither the length of the war nor mounting body counts was going to deter Ho Chi Minh's obsession to unite North and South. The Vietnamese were long suffering and their culture had accepted the inevitable consequences of warfare. America, on the other hand, found death and suffering a poor choice compared to living and living well, and perhaps that was a good thing. Aluminum coffins being wheeled off C-130s draped in American flags and photographed at municipal airports were difficult to justify.

The Soviets and Chinese had discovered a perfect partner in the North Vietnamese. Advising, training, and supplying Ho's forces was a small price to pay in exchange for the massive amounts of money spent and the ever increasing KIAs being sent back to the United States. The inability of the American politicians to either commit 100% of U.S. resources or bring the boys home was causing a disturbing climate on the home front.

For the Soviets and Chinese it was war by proxy, and the two puppet masters were manipulating to perfection. What could be better: no body bags returning home, no civilian upheaval, and a chance to field test their military hardware? All the benefits while the American people turned on themselves with anti-war and pro-war demonstrations. At the same time questions were being raised about the fairness of the draft system that seemed to take more than a fair share of blue collar, minority, and poor for draftees. There also developed a privileged group that worked the system for draft deferments based on bogus injuries and severe asthmatic conditions that mysteriously developed overnight. Some even left the country for safe haven in Canada and other nations rejoining the U.S. at a later and more convenient and safer time. All the while college enrollments swelled and draft deferments were dispensed like gold stars on the third day of 1st grade.

The tumult on the campuses and on the streets was just beginning. It must have been even more than the Soviets and Chinese could have hoped for while some Americans were being chased around Laos and Cambodia. Some who would never return.

With all the fine military gear the NVA had received, coupled with America's partial commitment to the war, SOG and their faithful air assets were left to slow the NVA's use of the Ho Chi Minh Trail that wound through Laos and Cambodia.

The peculiar concoction that SOG brought to the table confounded the NVA's use of the trail by adapting new tactics and using some of their own against them. SOG cobbled together some very interesting and dedicated military professionals. Lloyd Fisher, Bob Cavanaugh and Gilbert Hamilton were actually writing the books on this type of warfare dealing with the massive man superiority the NVA threw at them. If the NCOs were the cutting edge, they were quickly honing the new bloods in the person of company grade officers like Rod Hoepner, Gamble Dick and Bill Vowell.

SOG had to evolve over a short period of time not only to succeed but in order to survive. Rapidly training the mercenaries that were available at any given area was a monumental obstacle, yet the training was accomplished. Sadly, those mercenaries were later abandoned by the U.S. government. Our only real friends from Southeast Asia, they ultimately gave far more than they received.

SOG rolled up an impressive list of wounded, killed in action and missing in action as well. Lieutenant Bill Vowell noted in his writings that NCOs were dying "by the wheel barrel load" and that was just in the time he spent at Forward Operating Base # 1at Phu Bai. There could have been even more casualties, maybe even truck loads had it not been for the combined efforts of the crews like the Army's 191st 190th Attack Helicopter Company and men like Bill Whitney, Warrant Officer Bill Zanow and Warrant Officer Kent Woolridge.

It took a very special kind of man to sit in a single engine unarmed Cessna and hang out over a battle field where each of the enemy could reach and catch you with something as simple as an AK-47 rifle. Captain Kip Kippenhan did it; so did the pilot of Covey 57 and possibly others as well. They played a huge role in evening the odds SOG's men went up against each time they crossed the fence. Sitting in a lonely cockpit with only a radio microphone in hand and a list of air support possibilities in their heads, their decisions could mean all the difference. Where SOG went, Covey pilots followed, and from their darkened and lonely perch decisions were made. Real life or death decisions very much unlike what transpired in air-conditioned offices in Da Nang.

If not for one well-placed rocket propelled grenade, the Jolly Green rescue helos would have completed the rescue of Recon Team Flatfoot and a much happier result would have taken place. The spectacular and selfless action of Captain Gerald Young was reflected in his being awarded the Congressional Medal of Honor. Captain Jack McTasney and his Jolly crew succeeded in rescuing part of Recon Team Flatfoot and somehow managed to save all aboard their badly mauled helo. The Air Force also sent some very aggressive aviators flying their soon to be retired prop driven A-1Es. Keeping the NVA at bay with their well-placed ordnance, the pilots received a lengthy list of awards for their superior aviation over Hill 891.

The NVA presented a formidable opponent in both Laos and Cambodia. Over Hill 891 the NVA were especially aggressive and were present in superior numbers. However, it can be successfully argued that the SOG Recon Team and Hatchet Force combined with the Army and Air Force air units together shot the NVA off the face of the mountain. It might also be argued that the NVA withdrew to fight another day, satisfied to have created death and mayhem for those that did the same to them.

There can be little doubt that the NVA took horrendous casualties that no book will ever be able to confirm. Bulldog controlled the mountain by the end of their mission, if only by a hair. The Hatchet Force had been on the mountain when Captain Young was plucked from the grasp of the NVA. They had rescued Specialist 4 Jarvis and had him successfully transported back to Phu Bai unharmed. Several of Bulldog's Special Forces members, including Sergeant First Class Bob Cavanaugh, Second Lieutenant Rod Hepner and Master Sergeant Charles Minnicks were able to deny any useable American equipment by destroying it with explosives. In addition, Sergeants First Class Bell and Hamilton decimated an entire platoon of NVA with withering machine gun fire. That platoon would not participate in the TET offensive or any other offensive.

Finally, the five American KIAs were located and identified by sight recognition, eliminating the possibility they had been captured or labeled MIA. However, the technical and definitive identification that required a laboratory and skilled forensic anthropologist could not be done on the mountainside.

Lloyd Fisher and Ron Bock huddled together and agreed on some recommendations for Dr. Baker's team to explore. Hopefully, the scientists could now locate the remains of the five Americans, identify them and "the friggin mission" would be complete.

In a way Dr. Baker was much like Lloyd Fisher. She too was competitive and always in the pursuit of excellence. She had barged into the world of forensic science, a world largely inhabited by her male counterparts. Not to be denied, she had earned degrees from three separate universities and was committed to working in the field. Her hard charging style did not go unnoticed by the two former Green Berets. She was just the kind of professional they could respect and trust to bring a fitting conclusion to the 36 year-old mission. Both Sergeants expressed their admiration for Baker and she held them in the highest regard as well.

A base camp had been established for the scientists and their staff at Taoy. It was a 15 minute helo ride from the excavation site on Hill 891. The encampment had some tents, several block buildings, and a small restaurant run by some locals that featured large quantities of local staples, very well prepared and priced at bargain basement rates. The local population was largely made up of poor people who relied on their ability to adapt in order to survive.

Quickly Baker's team got busy on a site that promised to produce the remains of Kussick, Baxter, Maysey, Clay and Brower. The business of forensic anthropology is not what we have been led to believe by television's CSI Miami. Laotian mountainsides bear little resemblance to the white sand beaches of Miami. Baker's team found the mountainside to be very steep, up to a 20° slope in some places, and 37° in others. The slope bore a nasty gash on its east facing side that Dr. Baker referred to as a "wash." The wash had a funnel shape carved out by rapidly moving rainwater that arrived each year in the heart of the rainy season that had probably visited for decades if not longer.

There were no trees near the wash as the soil was not able to support them. There was a triple canopy jungle composed of ancient trees nearly 800 meters towards the bottom of the slope. Dr. Baker's notes also indicated that the area of interest was slightly more than 650 yards or 6 ½ football fields from top to bottom. There was some spotty wispy and weak vegetation in the form of elephant grass and bamboo that grew mainly along the perimeter of the wash. The soil contained rocks and clay both in large quantities.

Another interesting feature was a small Laotian village that went by the name Ban-Aho. It was located approximately 1 kilometer, or 3/5 of a mile, to the south of the excavation site. There were foot trails that led from Ban-Aho and passed very close to the excavation site.

The Hawaii-based scientists felt confident that they would be able to uncover at least some remains, if not a significant sample for the purposes of identification. But first there would be a great deal of back breaking labor to do with both time and money as factors. The search for the remains began with the examination of search and rescue records which included mission reports and radio traffic that occurred throughout the length of the incident. Because these reports were made under duress and the constant threat of danger, they lack specificity and at times are general in their descriptions. They were never intended to be scientific. Also, records and written material that pertained to operations into Laos and Cambodia were subject to destruction around 1975. Most of this information was used as corroboration and as a starting point.

Eye witnesses were also contacted, the most obvious being Lloyd Fisher and Ron Bock. One local villager was also sought, but he was away during the excavation. Few villagers would have wanted to expose themselves to the NVA or be near the air assault the Americans unleashed on Hill 891. This action was not a spectator sport and there were few places one would have deemed safe enough to observe from.

Technicians with metal detectors were deployed to locate the debris that fire fights often leave in their wake. It was also prudent to sweep for mines and unexploded ordnance lest there be another injury such as the one Sergeant First Class Osborne suffered in November of 1967. When strong signals were received by the operators they set up flags to indicate that spot for closer scrutiny. A pedestrian survey was also taken which employed team members to deploy to pre-designated areas and methodically eyeball their assigned territory and flag anything peculiar or of interest.

The excavation area was then organized into grids or squares that were 4 meters by 4 meters. This amounted to a 13 foot by 13 foot square. There were at least 100 of these marked out to be examined by the forensic team. The grid was then excavated 18 centimeters, approximately 7 inches deep, in U.S. measurement. The soil was then screened for artifacts and remains which included bones, teeth, etc. It was time consuming and tedious, and it was performed at a location that featured a steep slope, high heat, humidity, and a troop of hostile insects. In short, it was a very uncomfortable place to work.

Curiously enough, after all the necessary steps were followed by the forensic team, only a few clues were found to indicate a desperate struggle had taken place on Hill 891.

Earlier deployed parachutes had been found, and now the grids turned up some spent shell casings and bullets. It had been a promising start yet there were few if any parts found from the ill-fated HH-3 Jolly Green Giant. The massive helo had nearly disappeared from the face of the mountain.

Neither the NVA or the U.S. Air Force would have any use for helo parts that had been shot out of the sky, crashed, rolled, burned, and were blown up by American forces. Certainly no natural occurrence could have moved it. That left only one possibility. Dr. Baker theorized that the foot trail that led to the village of Ban-Aho had provided enough thoroughfare for some poor but enterprising salvagers to score some windfall profit from the helo's metal.

There had been many missions to recover the remains of American servicemen left unaccounted for in Southeast Asia. Dr. Baker had been on 10 or more herself. Each mission had its own set of circumstances, however, there was a common factor found in many excavations and that was the high levels of acidity contained in the soil. On Hill 891 no skeletal remains were ever found, and it is believed to be the acid levels that in concert with the heat and high humidity decimated the skeletal remains.

There was yet another culprit to blame for the remains not being located and that was the water that flowed over the soil gaining momentum as it rushed down the mountain. Bone fragments already lightened by the sun and acid were likely to have been washed downhill by the rushing water.

Dr. Baker, like everyone else who attempted to locate and recover the remains of the five Americans, felt the frustration of being unable to bring closure to the families and the professional satisfaction that her team was denied. It was the same feeling that many of the Hatchet Force and those that supported Bulldog shared with the team sent by JPAC.

There was yet another road block that occurred when the forensic team visited and worked on Hill 891. A Special Forces Lieutenant Colonel stationed in Laos oversaw the excavation site. Baker realized that her team needed to move further down the hill in order to be successful in locating whatever remains that had not been completely consumed by the acidic clay soil, wild animals, or the toll taken by the humidity, heat, and direct sunlight.

The Special Forces Lieutenant Colonel was not in favor of Baker's team expanding their excavation further down the slope. He claimed the site could be lengthened later in the spring by a forensic team that would replace the one currently at the site. Baker was quick to point out that delaying until spring may bring heavy runoff from the vegetation less wash. This could place a forensic team in a compromising position directly in the path where flood waters would be at their worst and possibly resulting in more fatalities on Hill 891. Dr. Baker was opposed to the officer's proposal. There was no guarantee that another attempt would be made to excavate following Baker's 2003 mission. There was no shortage of other promising sites that were equally worthy of investigation and also demanded funding.

Much like Hatchet Force Bulldog, Baker's team ran out of time and returned to Hawaii to be assigned other jobs and missions. These missions were equally important to other families and loved ones. Hill 891 was put on hold and continues to remain in that status.

The inability of both the search and rescue teams and the forensic teams to recover all or any of the five Americans was certainly affected by the NVA either directly or indirectly. Yet the most persistent and dogged obstacle to recovering American warriors was Hill 891. It deserved the title of mountain and it flexed its considerable muscle much like a mountain would.

Like the warriors and scientists that labored, sweat, bled, and shivered on its slope, the mountain seemed to possess the traits of having been trained. Like a veteran Olympic wrestler, the mountain offered up some slick moves and counter moves as well. In its bag of tricks, perhaps the most consistent at foiling each mortal team that dared to test it was by far its steepness. It absolutely refused to allow a helicopter to plant two skids on the ground simultaneously. Even when resting one skid on the ground, the pilots had to struggle to keep their rotors from striking the rocky mountainside.

Combatants and scientists alike noted the slickness of the mountainside, especially when even the slightest bit of moisture touched down. The soil consisting of heavy clay content caused slipping and leg weariness. It accumulated on boots making every step pure drudgery. For this very reason, Master Sergeant Fisher requested an H-34 helo equipped with a winch to lift the bodies off the mountainside. Since the helo could not land, it would be forced to hover and yet another crew would become a sitting duck. Two helos had already become smoking piles of junk with their crew's status at the time unknown.

A vicious cycle of events had been created on the mountainside. Those in command probably felt the need to break the cycle. The men on and above the mountain wanted to continue the match. Their competitive instincts and hearts could not face a stalemate or a loss.

Grappling with the wily old mountain proved a challenge for both professional soldier and learned scientists alike. With each mission the mountain featured an impressive array of changing hurdles to clear. The fog, mist, cold, and humidity tightened its grip on the remains of the five Americans and stubbornly refused to surrender them.

Much has been written to portray the NVA as the David during the conflict in Southeast Asia. They have been described as the cunning, resourceful, and motivated force. But if the NVA thought of Hill 891 as an ally they too would soon learn just how fickle the mountain could be. The NVA found themselves in a submission hold and were then put on their backs. The mountain had provided Bulldog's expert gunners with perfect camouflage and concealment and at the very least aided Sergeants

First Class Hamilton and Bell to riddle an entire NVA platoon with 7.62 mm projectiles that ruined an entire platoon's day.

Hill 891 was treacherous, fickle, and deadly and showed no allegiance to either the NVA or Americans. It wasn't even hospitable to its native Laotians. Bad guys, good guys, it recognized neither and it flat out refused to satisfy the American culture's desire to gain closure. Family had no meaning to 891. It didn't have feelings and wouldn't comply with the military custom of returning deceased warriors. If it was peace of mind Bulldog's men sought, they were not to receive it from the mountain.

Dr. Baker's team of fine professionals, like Bulldog, would only experience a modicum of the success they both desired and sought. They too were subject to the same old moves Hill 891 had applied to the NVA, Bulldog and the air crews. Baker's team received no preferential treatment being non-combatants. They, too, were treated to a dose of the mountain's steep terrain, sticky clay soil, and possibly the same questionable decisions by the brass as well. Despite the resistance the mountain threw up, the forensic team began to locate the shell casings and bullets that had been expended in November of 1967. The lack of Jolly Green parts had been explained and it appeared that the work at the excavation site was closing in on finishing the "friggin mission." If Baker's team could close the deal it would go a long way in filling the empty feeling that remained in the hearts of the men that risked their lives "cleaning up the mess."

But the mountain shrugged off and neutralized JPAC's heavyweights just as it had confounded the professional warriors. The shell casings and bullets did not lead to the discovery of any human remains. The mountain had allowed Baker's team to score a few points, but it cruelly put the scientists on their collective backs just as it had done to the combined search and rescue group.

While the scientists and the warriors of SOG have matured and in some cases grayed with age, the mountain continues to stand tall and remain as strong as it was in November of 1967. There is nothing in the foreseeable future that indicates the mountain will surrender or be forced to give up the remains of Joseph Kussick, Bruce Baxter, Ralph Brower, Eugene Clay or Larry Maysey.

To date JPAC has no plans to revisit Hill 891, however, should they change their plans 80 year old Lloyd Fisher stands ready for one final try to "complete the friggin mission,"

Estimated locations of American remains for REFNO 0902 in Samouay District, Salavan Province from information given by CSM(R) Lloyd Fisher and Mr. Ron Bock, members of the SAR Team that occupied the site in November 1967 after the crash. Information was provided during JFA 03-4L, 25-28 June 2003.

AWARDS RESULTING FROM ACTION ON HILL 891, LAOS, 1967

Combatant	Branch of Service	Rank	Specialty	Award
Sandies				
Aycock, Robert	U.S.A.F.	Major	Pilot A1-E	Silver Star
Jenks, Robert C.	U.S.A.F.	Major	Pilot A1-E	Silver Star
Kilbourne, Jimmy	U.S.A.F.	Major	Pilot A1-E	Silver Star
Leonard, Edward	U.S.A.F.	Major	Pilot A1-E	Silver Star
Hatchet Force Bulldog				
Bock, Ron	U.S.A. Special Forces	Sergeant	Medic-Hatchet Force	Silver Star
Cavanaugh, Robert	U.S.A. Special Forces	Sergeant First Class	Weapons	Bronze Star Purple Heart
Osborne, Erskine	U.S.A. Special Forces	Sergeant First Class	Demolition	Purple Heart
Recon Team Flatfoot				
Baxter, Bruce *	U.S.A. Special Forces	Master Sergeant	Leader Recon Team	Distinguished Service Cross
Fleming, Alan (Chips)	U.S.A. Special Forces	Lieutenant	0-2 Recon Team	Combat Infantryman Badge, Purple Heart
Kussick, Joseph *	U.S.A. Special Forces	Sergeant	R.O. Recon Team	Silver Star

Jolly Green 26

Brower, Ralph *	U.S.A.F.	Captain	Pilot	Air Force Cross
Clay, Eugene *	U.S.A.F.	Sergeant	Flight Engineer	Air Force Cross
Maysey, Larry *	U.S.A.F.	Sergeant	Pararescueman	Air Force Cross
Young, Gerald	U.S.A.F.	Captain	Pilot	Congressional Medal of Honor

Spartan 53

Whitney, William *	U.S.A.	Sergeant	Crew Chief, Huey	Distinguished Service Cross
Woolridge, Kent	U.S.A.	Warrant Officer	Pilot, Huey	Purple Heart
Zanow, William	U.S.A.	Warrant Officer	Pilot, Huey	Purple Heart

Jolly Green 29

Clearman, Jerry	U.S.A.F.	Captain	Pilot	Silver Star
Malone, Alvin	U.S.A.F.	Sergeant	Flight Engineer	Silver Star
McTasney, Jack	U.S.A.F.	Captain	Pilot	Air Force Cross
Stemple, John	U.S.A.F.	Sergeant	Pararescueman	Silver Star

* Killed as a result of hostile action on or near Hill 891, Laos, Southeast Asia, November, 1967.

GLOSSARY

A-1—Propeller driven fighter bomber first used in Korea
7th Air Force—Located at Tan Son Nhut—oversaw air operations in SEA. General Momyer was 7th AF Commander
ADF—Altitude density factor as it applies to helicopters
AGL—Above ground level as it applies to aircraft
AK-47—North Vietnam's standard rifle supplied by various countries. Still in use today
Alley Cat—Night time airborne command and control aircraft (EC-130) from Udorn Air Base, Thailand
Alpha One—Ready status for Jolly Green helicopters
ARVN—Army of the Republic of Vietnam (South Vietnam)
B-52—High altitude American bomber
Bingo—U.S. Air Force jargon for low on fuel
Blind Bat—Call sign for Air Force C-130 flare ship
Bodes—Cambodian mercenaries paid by the CIA
Boom Boom Girl—Vietnamese bar fly
Bulldog—Call sign for SOG Hatchet Force
Charlie—Viet Cong
CIA—Central Intelligence Agency
CIB—U.S. Army combat infantry badge
C-Rat—U.S. food rations—Vietnam era
Covey—call sign for U.S. Air Force spotter planes or FACS
Covey Rider—S.F. Sergeant assigned to Fac pilot as an advisor
Crown—Rescue Control Aircraft—(HC-130)
DAF—Density altitude factor—the effect of heat, humidity and altitude had on the ability of a helicopter to lift
E-Tool—small folding shovel carried by infantry
Exfiltrate—Removing small groups of soldiers from hostile areas

F-4 Phantom—U.S. strike aircraft
FAC—U.S. Air Force forward air controller
FE—Rescue helicopter flight engineer
Flak trap—Using downed aircraft as bait to bring in additional air assets, NVA tactic
Flare the Helicopter—Stop downward motion
Flatfoot—Call sign for SOG recon team
FNG—U.S. slang for fuckin new guys
FOB—Forward Operating Base used by SOG
Gladiator—U.S. Army attack helicopter call sign
Green Beanie—Derogatory term for Green Beret
Grunt—Marine rifleman
Gunfighter—F-4 fighter bomber from 366th Tactical Fighter Wing, Da Nang
H-34—U.S. helicopter, preceded the Huey
Halo—Jumping out of an aircraft at high altitude, opening a parachute at a low altitude
Hatchet Force—US. Special Forces led team used to search and recover Recon Teams in distress
HF—Hatchet Force, SOG rescue team
Hercules—U.S. Air Force C-130 versatile aircraft
Hi Performance—Jets
Hillsboro—Daytime airborne command post over Laos from Udorn Air Base, Thailand
Hooch—Any place a serviceman could stay dry
Huey—U.S. helicopter first used in Vietnam
Indig—Indigenous force or mercenary
Insertion—Placing small groups of soldiers into hostile areas
JTF-FA—Joint Task Force for full accounting. A scientific/investigative group formed to help bring closure to U.S. families whose loved ones were never to return home.
Jolly Green—U.S. Air Force rescue helicopter (also known as J.G.)
KIA—Killed in action
King—Search and Rescue controller call sign
Kingbee—H34 helicopter predecessor of Huey
LZ—Landing zone, generally applied to helicopters
M-1—World War II vintage rifle issued to mercenaries
M-15—Modified M-16 issued to Special Forces

M-16—Standard issue rifle for U.S. riflemen
M-26—U.S. issued hand grenade
M-60—Standard U.S. machine gun
MACV—Military Assistance Corp—Vietnam
MG—machine gun
Misty—Call sign for U.S. Air Force super sabers and FACs
MOS—Military occupational specialty
Newbie—U.S. jargon for inexperienced soldiers
NCO—Non commissioned officer (Sergeants)
NJSP—New Jersey State Police
NVA—North Vietnamese Army—regular troops
01, 02, OV-10—Slow flying, prop driven FACS
OPS—Military operations (U.S.)
PAVN—People's Army of Vietnam (North Vietnam)
Pipeline—U.S. Air Force jargon for PJ training
PJ—Pararescue man or 'para jumper', U.S. Air Force
PRC 25—Radio carried by U.S. forces in Vietnam. 23.5 lbs., a.k.a. "Prick 25"
PSP—Perforated steel plate
PZ—Pick up zone. Helicopter landing area for extraction
QC—Qualification Course—part of Special Forces training
Queen—Search and Rescue Coordination Center at Tan Son Nhut Air Base, Vietnam
Recon Team (RT)—Reconnaissance team
RON—Remain overnight position
RTAB—Royal Tai Air Base used by U.S. air assets in Thailand
RTB—U.S. Air Force jargon for return to base
RPG—Rocket propelled grenade used by NVA and Vietcong—supplied by China and the USSR.
Sandy—Call sign for U.S. Air Force A-E1 Sky Raiders
SAR—Search and rescue
SEA—Southeast Asia
Secret War—U.S. clandestine operations in Laos/Cambodia
SF—Special Forces, U.S. Army elite warriors
Silver Wings—Badge awarded to those that qualify in parachute training
Slick—Army helicopter dedicated for transportation

SMM—Sergeant Major Mafia—unofficial term applied to the sergeants who ran the Special Forces

SNAFU—Situation normal, all fucked up

SOG—Studies and observation group—an arm of the CIA

SOPC—Special Operations prep course, part of Special Forces training

Spartan—Call sign for U.S. A. Huey slick

Spook—A CIA operative

Swedish K—Sub machine gun made in Sweden

TOC—Tactical Operations Center area where decisions and information was distributed to those awaiting a mission

URC-10—U.S. issued survival radio for air crews

VNAF—Vietnamese Air Force (South Vietnam)

WO—Warrant Officer—hybrid rank that loosely combined an officer and an NCO (Army pilot)

BIBLIOGRAPHY

Published Sources

Burkett, B.G. & Glenna Whilley, "Stolen Valor," *Verity Press Inc.*, Dallas, TX, 1998.

Carlock, Chuck, "Firebird," *The Summit Publishing Group*, Arlington, TX, 1995.

Fall, Bernard, "Street Without Joy," *Stackpole Books*, Harrisburg, PA, 1961.

Lanning, Michael Lee & Dan Cragg, "Inside The V.C. and The N.V.A.," *Fawcett*, Columbine, NY, 1992.

McConnell, Malcolm, "Into The Mouth of The Cat," *W. W. Norton & Co.*, New York, NY, 1985.

Plaster, John L., "Secret Commandos," *Simon & Schuster*, New York, NY, 2004.

Plaster John L., "SOG," *Onyx Publishing*, New York, NY, 1998.

Prados, John, "The Blood Road," *John Wiley & Sons, Inc.*, New York, NY, 1998.

Sorley, Lewis, "Westmoreland," *Houghton Mifflin*, Harcourt, NY, 2011.

Periodicals

Guns and Ammo Magazine

Waugh, Billy, "Special Forces Days"